The F Staying in Touch

How Our Loved Ones Contact Us and How We Can Contact Them

By

Roberta Grimes

Foreword by Gary E. Schwartz, Ph. D.

ISBN Paperback: 978-1-7374106-2-1
ISBN ePub: 978-1-7374106-3-8

GR

Greater Reality Publications
23 Payne Place
Normal, IL 61761
www.greaterreality.com
800 690-4232
bookorders@greaterreality.com

Contact the Author: www.robertagrimes.com

By the Author

Liberating Jesus

My Thomas

The Fun of Dying

The Fun of Staying in Touch

The Fun of Growing Forever

The Fun of Living Together

The Fun of Meeting Jesus

(Children's Picture-Book)

This book is gratefully dedicated
to each of the thousands of unsung scholars
whose wonderful work made it possible.

Contents

Foreword by Gary E. Schwartz, Ph.D.

The Fun of Staying in Touch is a beautifully written treasure of personal stories, historical information, humor, and wisdom about staying in touch. Some of what Roberta Grimes writes has been scientifically documented, some is based upon carefully researched historical accounts, and some is her own amazing experiences. It is in the very nature of our after-death communications that they are personal and anecdotal. But the fact that the dead survive has been well established, including through extensive documentation in my own laboratory, and each of the kinds of signs that Grimes describes has been repeatedly reported.

As you will find as you read this delightful book, it really can be fun to stay in touch with those "on the other side." I first learned this lesson from my dear friend Susy Smith, both before and after she "crossed over." When I first met Susy, she was 85 years old. She quickly became a mentor and an inspiration for me, fondly calling me her "illegitimate grandson." Susy told me she had developed the capacity to communicate with her deceased mother, Elizabeth, and that communication had continued almost nightly for more than 40 years. She was happily staying in touch, just as this book suggests. Susy also believed that she had developed a close professional and personal relationship with Professor William James, M.D., of Harvard University, a relationship that had begun decades after he had physically died. Professor James had been an internationally recognized scholar in experimental psychology, which included pioneering research on life after death. Amazingly, long before I met Susy, she had written two books in collaboration with what she claimed was Professor James's spirit, the first of which, *The Book of James,* had been a best-seller in the 1970s.

i

As a serious academic scientist with a Ph.D. from Harvard University and on the faculties of Harvard, Yale, and now the University of Arizona, I couldn't take Susy's claims at face value. But I was intrigued, so I conducted controlled research with Susy and with a number of other mediums that provided overwhelming evidence that the mediums were indeed in contact with the dead. We established that staying in touch after death is possible, as I revealed in my 2002 book, *The Afterlife Experiments*. Susy told me often that she couldn't wait to die so she could prove she was still here, and since her death she has been as good as her word. My wonderful friend still continues to assist me from the other side in my ongoing research into how we can better stay in touch with our dead loved ones.

Not everyone can have contact with someone like Susy Smith, whose eternal friendship I treasure. But with the help of this little book, you can begin your own journey into communicating with loved ones you had thought were lost to you. I hope you enjoy *The Fun of Staying in Touch* as much as I have!

Gary E. Schwartz, Ph.D., is Professor of Psychology, Medicine, Neurology, Psychiatry, and Surgery at the University of Arizona, and Director of the Laboratory for Advances in Consciousness and Health. His books include The Afterlife Experiments, The Truth about Medium, and The Sacred Promise.

Introduction

"The statistical probability that organic structures and the most precisely harmonized reactions that typify living organisms would be generated by accident, is zero."

—Ilya Prigogine, Physicist and Chemist,
winner of the 1977 Nobel Prize in Chemistry

"In considering the value of evidence for supernormal phenomena the importance of the cumulative character of the evidence must be taken into account. It is the undesigned coincidence of witnesses who have had no communication with each other that constitutes its value taken as a whole, whilst a single case may be doubtful or disproved, just as a single stick may be broken but a faggot may defy all our attempts at breaking a bundle of sticks."

—Sir William Barrett in *Deathbed Visions*
(1926)

"Ask, and it will be given to you; seek, and you will find; knock, and the door will be opened to you. For everyone who asks receives; he who seeks finds; and to him who knocks, the door will be opened."

—Jesus (MT 7:7–8)

"First they ignore you, then they laugh at you, then they fight you, then you win."

—Mahatma Gandhi

his is such an exciting time to be alive! After thousands of years during which humankind has been struggling to try to make sense of things, the truth about what we are, what reality is, and what actually is going on apparently is now being revealed. And it is going to change everything! We now know that you are an eternal being. You never began, and you never will end. The material reality in which you think you live is just a small part of a greater reality that is even now coming into view. And it is all good! We now know that you and everyone you love are together forever and safe in everlasting arms.

But for many people, even that is not the best news. No, the very best news of all is the fact that we are entering an age in which communication between the living and the dead will become ever easier. Things are happening in this field so quickly that I have hesitated to write this book, since to talk about the current state of play feels rather like describing a ball in flight. But it is important that you know what is going on. Our intention is to begin with a stake in the ground and then to update this book as necessary, which means that if the edition you are reading is more than five years old, there may be a later version available.

The dead have always been much more aware of us than we are of them. They have been trying for millennia to get our attention, if only to assure us that those we love have survived their deaths. There are reasons why the dead have had so much difficulty making their presence known, some of which have to do with the nature of reality itself and some of which have to do with human nature. When the leaders of mainstream science and mainstream Christianity have spent the past two thousand years battling over which of them possesses the truth, they both have naturally been unwilling to consider the possibility that neither of them has it right.

We are blessed to live in an age in which old beliefs are reaching what seem to be their natural dead ends. And as the old theistic and atheistic belief systems lose their strangleholds on our flow of information, more and more people are venturing into the vast and fertile valley of afterlife evidence that has accumulated between mainstream Christianity and mainstream science over the past two centuries. Working independently, these pioneering researchers are assembling an understanding of reality that is consistent with both quantum physics and the teachings of Jesus. How amazing is that? It turns out that scientists and religionists have long possessed portions of the truth, but in ignoring so much important evidence, each of them has missed the big picture. **As you will see, the truth about reality is beyond-belief wonderful!** And it is about to become common knowledge. We do indeed live in exciting times.

Of course, advocates for mainstream Christianity and mainstream science have substantial interests to protect, so as information becomes ever more widely available, their impulse will be to fight its dissemination. In an effort to minimize that, here is a message for each:

> • **To Christians:** I know of no one in the field of afterlife research who wants to interfere with your beliefs.
> • **To Scientists:** Researchers in the field of afterlife studies are delighted to share with you what they are learning. The information that can be gleaned from the evidence that you have been walking past will very much enhance your own efforts to better understand reality.
> • **To people still trying to murder this baby in its cradle:** Your day is past. Scientific debunkers have managed to mischaracterize the afterlife evidence sufficiently to delay this breakthrough for a hundred years, but the sea cannot be held back forever. Eventually the truth will win.

This book is meant to be an overview for those with little knowledge in this field. Rather than footnotes, it includes a brief study guide and also a comprehensive list of resources that you might use to duplicate my research. And if you are curious about the place from which the dead are communicating with us, you might read *The Fun of Dying* for a similar overview of the death process and the glorious realities that we enter at death.

It may surprise you to learn that we have been receiving abundant, consistent, and independently verified communications from the dead for nearly two hundred years. Even one such proven communication from someone who is documented to be dead should have settled the question of whether or not our minds survive our deaths, and by now we have many hundreds of them. **It is no longer possible for an open-minded person who examines the best evidence to have any doubt that the dead survive.**

Sadly, though, for more than a century, both mainstream scientists and mainstream Christians have done all they could to disparage these proven communications from the dead and to demonize those who investigate them. It is little wonder that what is the greatest news in human history has been hidden under a bushel for so long. I came across this information only because I had had two extraordinary experiences of light in childhood, so I knew there was *something* behind the curtain. I wanted to figure out what it was. And because I knew what had happened to me was real, I wouldn't settle for comforting pap. I wanted the truth! So I was (and remain) highly skeptical of each new bit of afterlife evidence. It took me decades of studying communications from the dead and relevant aspects of mainstream science before I was convinced that I had figured things out.

As you begin to learn the truth for yourself, you will find that the war against it continues. The greater reality that we enter at death is so amazingly different from this limited material universe that scientists trying to protect their careers have long used three dishonest techniques in an effort to keep you from wondering about it:

1. **They ignore the afterlife evidence.** This worked for the entire twentieth century. If scientists and the news media won't talk about something, then obviously it must not exist. The rise of the Internet has scotched this method, but scientific stonewalling explains why what has been known among researchers for more than a century is only now coming to your attention.

2. **They try to debunk the afterlife evidence.** With more people now taking the afterlife evidence seriously, some self-appointed defenders of the scientific faith have adopted a more aggressive technique. These folks generally call themselves skeptics, but their whole focus is on finding some way to explain a single aspect of some unusual phenomenon, to prove fraud, or otherwise to discredit whatever elements of afterlife research might be catching the public's eye. All of us should be skeptical! But anyone who calls himself a skeptic and then proceeds to demonstrate a minimal understanding of some phenomenon while he tries to explain it away is a debunker. Ignore him.

3. **They assert without support that some afterlife-related phenomenon has been debunked, or some researcher is a fraud.** It is easy now to debunk the debunkers. Thanks to the Internet, so much good information has become so widely available that the efforts of debunkers look amateurish. In desperation, those who would deny you these truths have taken to declaring without analysis or support that phenomena and researchers have been debunked or have been proven to be fraudulent. So widespread has this practice become among online encyclopedias and science-defender websites that any

resource that declares that anything has been debunked should be presumed to be lying to you until your own research has proven otherwise.

The fact that mainstream scientists and their partisans still refuse to investigate the afterlife evidence as they might investigate any other interesting phenomenon surprises me, frankly. The search for the truth is not a game to be won, but rather it is a shared effort by all of us to better understand what is going on. The longer they lie about the afterlife evidence, the more our most trusted sources of information are going to damage their own credibility, and knowing that saddens me. Their continued stonewalling means that humankind's dawning understanding of the fact that our minds are eternal is going to be a bottom-up effort. Those who should have been the leading discoverers of these truths will in the end be the last to acknowledge them.

Nothing that is said here is based on anyone's beliefs or dogmas. As should be true of every open-minded investigation of the truth, everything said in this book can be found in original source material or comes from trusted researchers. When I guess at something, I will tell you it's a guess. You have spent your life trying to make sense of competing theistic and atheistic belief systems. The least you deserve now is to have the facts presented to you without a beliefs-based gloss.

Some readers of *The Fun of Dying* have said that they would like to know more about how we can live lives on earth that will let us enjoy our very best eternal lives. For them, *The Fun of Growing Forever* is the third volume in this trilogy. As you will see, the best is yet to come!

Dead communicators tell us that it was never intended that physical death should come between loved ones. And thanks to the efforts of dedicated researchers now living on both sides of the veil, our illusory separation seems to be ending.

Chapter One

Why is Communication Between the Dead and the Living so Difficult?

"I regard consciousness as fundamental. I regard matter as derivative from consciousness. We cannot get behind consciousness. Everything that we talk about, everything that we regard as existing, postulates consciousness."

—Max Planck, winner of the 1918
Nobel Prize in Physics

"The distinction between past, present and future is only a stubbornly persistent illusion."

—Albert Einstein, winner of the 1922
Nobel Prize in Physics

"The Universe begins to look more like a great thought than like a great machine."

—Physicist, Astronomer and Mathematician Sir James Jeans

"A new command I give you: Love one another. As I have loved you, so you must love one another."

—Jesus (JN 13:34)

"All you need is love, love. Love is all you need."

—The Beatles

We have nearly two hundred years of abundant and consistent communications from the dead that tell us in considerable detail what happens at death and what the afterlife is like. When they are taken together and combined with some insights from mainstream science, these communications give us a picture of reality that is very different from the reality that we think we see. It is too early to say for certain, but there is considerable evidence now that there is no such thing as "solid" matter. Quantum physicist Max Planck was exactly right.

What then is real?

It is impossible to fully understand or express any of this in human terms, and what I say here is limited just to aspects of reality that bear on communication between the dead and the living. With those caveats, let's talk about what open-minded researchers are learning about the nature of reality.

MIND IS ALL THAT EXISTS

Apparently, the basis of reality is an infinitely powerful and infinitely creative energy-like potentiality without size or form that is alive in the sense that your mind is alive, and is highly emotional and therefore probably self-aware. That's it. That is all there is. You might call this energy-like potentiality Consciousness. You might with justification call it God, although that name carries a host of misleading religious connotations. In honor of Max Planck, the father of quantum physics and a primary proponent of the theory that human consciousness is primary and pre-existing, I have taken to calling it Mind. Your own mind is inextricably part of Mind. Your mind is not just made by Mind, but it *is* Mind. It is every bit as creative, as powerful, as emotional, as without size or form. If you are using the term "God," then your mind is part of God.

Stop and think about that for a moment.

One reason I am reluctant to refer to the base creative potentiality as "God" is that we are taught that God expresses a range of emotions. The potentiality at the base of all reality seems to express just one emotion, and that is the intense affinity that you and I experience as love.

We are used to thinking of our minds and souls as different things. I have seen experts define mind, soul, and spirit separately, but there is as yet no accepted set of definitions. For our purposes it doesn't matter. The evidence that I have seen indicates that the base creative force includes your mind, and your mind includes your soul and spirit. We will be using the terms interchangeably from here on.

Your mind is so complex that I don't think anyone alive understands it. It is clear, though, that just a part of your mind is accessible to your awareness while you are in a body. Much of it—perhaps most of it—is what scientists call your subconscious mind, but you and I might call it your superconsciousness or your oversoul. Your mind is vast, it is eternal, and it is powerful. So therefore:

> • **Nurturing your mind is a responsibility.** You are living in it forever! In my case, knowing these truths has meant no more cruel or violent entertainments and no unkind thoughts. I practice learning to love and forgive as if my life depended on it.
>
> • **The dead live with expanded and more powerful minds.** One of the many things that we don't know is how much more of their minds the dead can access, but clearly their reach is greater than ours. They can use their minds to manipulate our reality in ways that for you and me are impossible.
>
> • **Your mind is not generated by your brain.** Instead, your brain is something like a two-way radio in the head of a

meat-robot. Think of Jake's blue body in the movie *Avatar*. While the real you is safe in eternal Mind, your awareness is sufficiently connected to this alien body in an alien place to be able to move it and to pick up whatever its sensory organs are detecting. That's it! That is how little the real you is connected to this material universe, and how little your temporary body here matters.

Where your mind actually is, there is no matter and there is no time or space. Matter, with its associated energy and the associated concepts of time and distance, are all just aspects of this Mind-created material universe. Physicists tell us that the universe probably began in a Big Bang that expanded it from the size of a pencil-dot to its present apparently infinite size. How likely is that? For so much matter to have come from nothing makes no sense to you and me unless we realize that the universe is something like a thought. The fact that everything we think of as real is like a complex thought in eternal Mind is an important concept for us to grasp if we want to make sense of how afterlife communication might work.

Time is a constant only in this material universe. People living in the afterlife levels of reality can choose to experience time, but it doesn't rule their lives as it rules ours. It is for the dead both optional and elastic. There is no such thing as objective time, and without objective time your mind is eternal. That is true by definition.

MIND HAS CONSTRUCTED A MULTI-LAYERED SET OF MATERIAL-SEEMING REALITIES

The dead consistently describe seven-ish additional realities that exist precisely where this one is, and are separated from this material universe only by their higher rates of spiritual vibration.

We have no way of knowing whether these eight or so primary realities are all that exist, and I have a suspicion there are many more; but again, for our purposes it doesn't matter. Our minds and the minds of those we love exist eternally in these levels of mind-created reality, and we move among the levels according to what amount to the laws of spiritual physics.

The easiest way for you to envision the multi-level greater reality that the dead describe is to think of your mind as a television set. The distinction among these various realities is based upon their rates of spiritual vibration, just as the difference between television Channels Four and Seven is based on their different vibratory frequencies. Some of these levels of post-death reality are as solid-seeming as this one is. And as is true of all the channels that your TV can access, all these energy-levels of reality exist in the same place. Each level also has apparently infinite gradations of signal within that larger level's vibratory rate, and that detail allows each of us to have unique experiences in individual bodies.

So at this moment, your eternal mind is tuned to that particular body on this material level of reality. It is that simple. When you die, your mind will change channels and tune to the vibratory frequency of a new body at a higher vibratory level, and it will there pick up a whole new solid reality.

There is evidence that this material universe is at the lowest vibratory frequency—it is something like Channel One—but nobody knows that for sure. We do know that in order to keep our powerful minds from messing with the matter on this level, there is a mathematics-based, clockwork sort of physics that operates here. Try moving matter here with your mind. You can't do it. Minds can affect matter on other vibratory levels of reality because everywhere beyond this material universe, the physics that governs reality is consciousness-based. The quantum physics that Max Planck and his fellows discovered more than a century ago seems to be a kind of plug that connects the Newtonian physics of this material universe with the mind-controlled physics of most of reality.

The levels of reality that we enter at death seem as solid to their inhabitants as this one seems to us, with the wonderful difference that on those levels, the matter can be created and manipulated by the minds of their more advanced inhabitants.

LOVE IS WHAT DETERMINES SPIRITUAL DEVELOPMENT

Here is where we may lose a few readers. I understand how corny this will sound to some, and how too-good-to-be-true it will feel to others, but I don't make the rules. The afterlife evidence consistently and overwhelmingly reveals that the greatest sages in human history, including notables as varied as Jesus and the Beatles, have been right all along. **Love is all you need.**

It is a fact of the infinitely powerful energy-like potentiality that we here call Mind, of which each of our minds is an integral part, that the better it expresses the affinity that human beings in bodies experience as love, the higher is its vibratory rate. That is an oversimplification, but for our purposes it is good enough. After death, the minds of beings whose loving faculties are better developed live at higher vibratory frequencies—at higher channels, if you will—although they can readily lower their personal vibrations to visit those living at lower levels. For less loving beings to visit higher vibratory levels is impossible. These less-developed souls tell us that the more intense vibrations at higher levels are unbearable for them to experience. But since going to lower vibratory levels is easy for non-material beings, for millennia there have been dead people who were visiting their grieving loved ones on earth and desperate to reassure them that everything was fine.

Most of the inhabitants of the higher vibratory levels of reality of which we are aware are people who have occupied material bodies at least once. They are our dead. And I will here refer to them as "dead" because in our matter-obsessed culture, death has gotten an undeservedly bad rap. In fact, a properly-executed death is perhaps the best time of your life, and most of your eternal existence is lived gloriously as a dead person in realities that are far more wonderful than your most optimistic imaginings. So death is a good thing!

Let's use the word cheerfully.

PUTTING IT ALL TOGETHER

Think again of those television signals always ready in the room around you. They all exist together in the same place, just waiting for you to turn on your television set and pick up one of them. You might then choose another channel, and another and another, all of which are seemingly solid realities that exist simultaneously in that spot, but are undetectable without a TV. That is the difficulty and the promise of afterlife communication. The dead are exactly where we are, but you might say that their minds are tuned to Channel Four, while our minds are on Channel One.

Let's here summarize what all of this means from the perspective of afterlife communication:

- The only thing that exists is an infinitely powerful and highly emotional energy-like potentiality of which all human minds are an integral part, and from which as something like a thought comes all of what we think of as real.

- The eternal minds of our dead loved ones are exactly where we are, but they are tuned to a higher vibratory or frequency level.

- Minds at higher levels are easily able to visit lower levels, so the dead are much more aware of us than we are of them.

So near, and yet so far! We all are eternally part of Mind. Our minds remain connected with the minds of the dead, but we are living on different planes of reality. Imagine your Channel Five newsman trying to communicate with your Channel Seven newsman live, on air, and without electronics and you can better appreciate the problem. We all are on nearly the same frequency, true, but where energy levels are concerned, close is not enough.

When we talk about developing ways to communicate with minds on higher vibratory levels of reality, four big caveats also must be mentioned:

1. **Not all of the dead are able to be in touch with us.** Rarely, the newly-freed minds of the dead can go off-track for a time, and until they have completed their transition to their new bodies on a higher vibratory plane, they are unlikely to be able to communicate with us. Or they may be unwilling to communicate. The dead remain the same people they were in life, and since communication is a two-way street, we can't talk with them unless they want that connection.

2. **Time and other differences can further complicate communication.** We are obsessed with time in this clockwork universe, but where the dead reside there is no objective time. And in order to communicate with us, our dead loved ones have to lower their rate of vibration to be very close to our own. There are other impediments, too, that we will discuss in connection with a few of the most cutting-edge communication methods. Fortunately, dead researchers are working hard to solve all the problems they see.

3. **The intentions of researchers are all-important.** Since mind-energy is a highly emotional as well as an infinitely powerful potentiality, only open-minded researchers have a chance of achieving success in this field. Quantum physicists understand that the intentions of researchers can affect the results of their experiments, and what is true in quantum physics is true in spades when it comes to working with the minds of the dead. Openminded, objective curiosity is essential. Closedminded skeptics and debunkers get nowhere.

4. **Grief can act as a barrier to communication.** Here is a sad piece of irony! Hatred, anger, fear, and other negative emotions can make communication with the dead more difficult. Grief is among the strongest of negative emotions, and as such it seems to make effective communication between the dead and the living nearly impossible. It is imperative that you convince yourself soon after a death that your loved one is alive and fine. Get your grief tamped down to a wistful sadness, because the most effective communication tends to happen fairly soon after a death. If you are still wallowing in grief a year later, then in your case communication with that particular dead loved one may not happen.

A WORD ABOUT COINCIDENCE

Many of the signs of their survival that the dead have been giving us for millennia might be explained as amazing coincidences if the dead were not telling us through mediums that what we have experienced was their handiwork. Indeed, some of our dead friends insist that there is no such thing as coincidence, but everything that seems coincidental is engineered from a higher level of reality. I don't know about that, but I do know that the odds against chance for a specific set of events are often surprisingly long. For example, finding one penny means nothing. Finding dozens of pennies in various random places over two days' time soon after a loved one's death when you haven't been finding pennies either before or since is almost certainly not coincidental, since the odds against chance for it are prohibitive.

When it comes to spontaneous signs from the dead, the possibility of coincidence is ever-present. Many of these signs are so spectacular, though, that it is impossible for all of them to be coincidence. An honest statistician would find that some of these signs carry odds against chance in the multiple millions. My task here is not to offer proof, but rather to summarize for you what your own research would indicate. Of course, I don't expect you to take my word for anything. Instead, if this field interests you, I urge you to begin with the eight core books in Appendix I and move on to the resources in Appendix II. Discovering these truths for yourself can be a wonderful hobby!

MY EXAMPLES

It was only as I began to write this book that I realized that some of the most amazing signs from the dead that I have to share with you have happened to me personally. Apparently, the dead friends who have been nagging me to write about signs realize that I am skeptical of anything that I have not personally experienced. Most afterlife researchers are skeptics, actually. We have found parts of one gigantic truth, and since we know that the rest of what is true must still be out there, we won't settle for less. So in recent years, I have been given a set of wonderful signs that I will share with you under their appropriate categories. I experienced these events myself, so I can swear to you they actually happened.

THE DEAD CAN MANIPULATE OUR REALITY

People at higher vibratory levels of reality have always been very aware of the living, so apparently there have long been dead researchers working out ways to communicate to their living loved ones the fact of their survival. In the process, they have learned to use their minds to manipulate our reality. The next section of this book is devoted to cataloguing these types of signs from the dead, most of which are intended to convey some variant of a single message: we are alive, all is well, and when you die you will join us in a beautiful and loving new world. Following the first section detailing signs from the dead, the second section of this book is a summary of some of the ways in which the living can initiate communication with the dead, ranging from the ancient and familiar to the cutting-edge.

Human minds are eternal. Human love is forever. And now, thanks to the work of brilliant and dedicated researchers, both living and dead, we are at last learning how to stay in touch with those we love, even when someone's bodily death temporarily seems to get in our way.

How the Dead Contact Us

Chapter Two

Physical Signs

"This most beautiful system of the sun, planets and comets, could only proceed from the counsel and dominion of an intelligent and powerful Being."

—Sir Isaac Newton

"Our experience of separation may be an illusion of consciousness."

—Albert Einstein, winner of the
1922 Nobel Prize in Physics

"As the soul lives in the earth-life, so does it go to spirit-life. Its tastes, its predilections, its habits, its antipathies, they are with it still. It is not changed save in the accident of being freed from its body."

—Imperator, through William Stainton
Moses in *Spirit Teachings* (1883)

"I tell you the truth, if anyone says to this mountain, 'Go, throw yourself into the sea,' and does not doubt in his heart but believes that what he says will happen, it will be done for him."

—Jesus (MK 11:22-23)

*T**he dead have always been eager to assure us of their happy survival.** What seems to have been happened during all those millennia of post-death frustration was that dead people with better-developed minds experimented with manipulating our reality. As they found methods that worked, they began to teach them to the newly-dead, so eventually it seems to have become a part of the natural death process: you transitioned, you sent what amounted to postcard notices of your safe arrival, and then you went on to enjoy the glorious post-death realities.

Many of the ways in which the dead contact us seem to have ancient roots. That will become clearer to you as you learn about the most common post-death signs. We are told that there are groups of dead experts who assist new arrivals in making these signs happen, and apparently the more spiritually developed among the newly-dead can learn the techniques for themselves pretty quickly.

Some of the most common signs from the dead are physical manifestations. Stuff turns up. No one knows how these objects are made to appear, but some of them are probably *apports*: they are small objects dematerialized at another time and place and rematerialized wherever we are. People who have seen apports arriving tell us that they can appear in air and drop noisily to a table or onto the ground. And they arrive here fresh from somewhere else. For example, a sixty-year-old newspaper can arrive looking newly printed, but then yellow and age from here.

The list of physical manifestations by the dead that is given here is not exhaustive. These are just the most common ways in which the dead are known to send us physical signs of their survival, and some of them are so subtle that even if you think you have spotted a sign, you won't be sure about it until after you have verified it with your dead loved one through a medium. Each time you experience something that might be a sign, thank your dead loved one! Just say, "Thanks, Mom, please do it again," and go on about your day. Speaking aloud to the dead is important. The positive energy produced by your verbal communication is of tremendous benefit to the process, so never mind whatever stares you might get. Speak your thanks aloud every time. Most of the dead will stop giving us signs pretty quickly if we won't acknowledge their efforts.

SMALL OBJECTS

The most common small objects that the dead give us are coins. People start finding coins in the same denomination—pennies, mostly—or they find repeated clusters of the same set of coins. The coins sent as signs will sometimes bear a significant date, such as a birth or death year or a wedding year. They tend to turn up in places where they shouldn't be: not just on the pavement, but also on tabletops, on shelves, in drawers and empty pockets. One penny randomly found means nothing, but if soon after a death you are repeatedly finding coins, then that is probably not random. One woman pried open a long-stuck drawer in her grandmother's dresser soon after the woman died and found it empty, except for a brand-new penny.

Some of these small objects that seem to appear from out of nowhere are not coins. They can be long-lost jewelry, photos, old ticket stubs, or just about anything that reminds you of a dead loved one.

I received one wonderful little sign two days after my mother's death. I was babysitting my three-year-old grandchild when she came to where I was sitting and put something into my hand. What she had given me was a little metal angel that had "Your guardian angel is watching over you" engraved into its skirt. Now, I don't think that was an apport. Although no one in the family recognized it, I imagine she had found it somewhere in that household of four active children. What is significant is the fact that in the whole of her life to date, this was the only time she ever has handed me anything without comment and walked away. Impressing their intentions on the minds of animals and people is one of the things the dead have learned to do well.

FEATHERS

Feathers are a type of small object so commonly used by the dead as signs that they deserve to be considered by themselves. We all find random feathers now and then, so finding one or two along the way maybe every week or two should not be considered significant. But if you have recently lost a loved one and you are suddenly finding feathers everywhere, either feathers of one kind of bird that was important to your dead loved one or maybe all kinds of feathers in unlikely spots, then you should try to collect them and say "Thank you" every time. One woman told me that after a loved one died, she was finding feathers all through the day for a while, including a bright-blue ostrich plume on the hood of her car.

Some of the dead who leave feathers seem to stick to it for longer than is true of most other kinds of signs. I have heard from people who were still finding significant numbers of feathers even many years after a loved one's death.

INSECTS

Right up there with coins and feathers are insect-signs. Nearly all the insects used by the dead as signs are dragonflies and butterflies, perhaps because those are the insects that we are most likely to notice. They even can appear out of season or in spectacular insect-clouds.

The minds of the dead seem to be able to command insects with astonishing precision. One substitute who was called in to work after a teacher's unexpected death reported that on her first morning in the classroom, a yellow butterfly flitted in and went from student to student up and down the rows, alighting on each small head in turn, after which it flew out an open window. One very powerful being has made dragonflies his specialty, and once when his family was having a cookout, he filled the backyard thickly with dragonflies for that whole afternoon. Dragonflies and butterflies that alight on people and stay on a shirt or even on a hand, seemingly unafraid, are often reported.

My own set of insect-signs was the most surprising I have heard described. I began to see butterflies and dragonflies as soon as the day after my mother's death, but never more than a few at a time. Then, a couple of weeks after she died, in the heat of an August morning, I looked out at my backyard and found it full of dragonflies. Full! And not a butterfly to be seen. There were many hundreds of dragonflies of every size and type cruising in clouds, alighting here and there, and the show went on for that whole day. Sometimes there were no more than a dozen or so, but then again repeatedly there would appear a yard-wide mass of what looked like thousands of dragonflies, always limited to just my backyard. I thanked my mother repeatedly. What an astonishing, life-affirming gift!

The following morning when I looked outside, I saw no dragonflies at all, but I found my yard filling with butterflies. For hours I had clouds of many hundreds of butterflies of all sizes and kinds flitting everywhere in glorious profusion. At this point I was overwhelmed. I sat out on my deck in hundred-degree heat for much of the afternoon and watched that amazing show.

My mother was not quite through. The next day, I had dragonflies again, just a few in the morning, but by the afternoon my backyard was again filled with clouds of dragonflies. There were no butterflies at all.

Wow, three days in a row! I couldn't wait to see what Mom would do next. The following morning, though, there were no insects. Not so much as a beetle. Just before noontime, I stepped outside again to check for insects, and a single dragonfly together with a single orange butterfly flew together side by side in front of my face from right to left. Apparently, that was her signature. No matter how often I looked, there were no insects of note to be seen in my backyard for the rest of that whole summer.

BIRDS AND ANIMALS

As the dead are readily able to command insects, so they also seem to be able pretty easily to command birds and animals. Wild creatures have learned to avoid human beings, so you can consider any bird or wild animal that seems to be unafraid of you to be potentially under the control of your dead loved one. Each such instance may be a sign, so you should speak your gratitude while asking for more.

One common sign from the dead is birds flying in front of our windshields. Birds that swoop close to you when you are out in the open should similarly be considered possible signs. Or you might see a bird where it shouldn't be, perhaps out of season or out of its natural range. One woman who brought her father's body north from Florida one winter to be buried in his family's Long Island plot reported that for several days in a row when she visited her father's gravesite she was greeted by a beautiful white Florida crane.

Freakishly unafraid birds or small animals of any kind might be signs. There was one recent summer afternoon when a huge owl came and perched on a light while a celebration of someone's life was underway on the patio below it, and the owl stayed there until the last guest had left. A squirrel that approaches you as if it knows you, a mouse or a lizard that looks you in the eye, should be noticed and mentioned aloud to your loved one on the chance that perhaps it was meant as a sign.

One man who died as a young adult was for years giving his family bright-red cardinals as his sign. Then eventually his grandfather died, and Grandpa's favorite bird had been the blue jay. Their bereaved mother and daughter was tremendously comforted to look out her window one morning and see what would otherwise have seemed impossible: a bright-red cardinal and a brilliant blue jay were perched together on a nearby branch!

We are told by our dead loved ones that they produce insect-signs by essentially herding insects and groups of insects with their mind-energy, and they impress their thoughts on the brains of larger creatures to prompt them to behave in certain ways. They even can influence people to say or do certain things. They can prompt us to think of the dead loved one or to turn and notice something, and we will have no idea what is going on.

MANIPULATING OUR REALITY

There is a category of signs from the dead that blows your mind when you experience it, and frankly until you experience one of these signs, you are going to find it hard to believe they can happen. But they do in fact happen often.

- **Impressions.** Sometimes a widow or widower will feel the springs on the bed compress where a spouse once slept, and some even report that they can see the depression in the mattress happen when their dead spouse gets into bed beside them. Animals seem to be especially good at producing impressions in bedclothes: many who have lost a pet to which they were especially close will report seeing the little paw-impressions appear on the bed and then the depression appear where the animal once slept.

- **Physical Mischief.** Some of our dead loved ones will make pictures go crooked repeatedly, will tip photos off tables or mantels, will hide and then bring back significant objects, and in other ways will play little pranks that would be significant to the bereaved. This sort of thing seems to happen often, but the thought that the dead can move objects makes people uncomfortable so most bereaved folks will keep these stories to themselves. One widow told me a wonderful tale in this vein only after I had told her I was writing this book and she and I had chatted for a while. She said that there was a large family picture hanging on a wall of her home. **Two weeks after her husband's death, while she watched it happen, the picture had lifted off its hanger, flipped in the air, and landed on the carpet.** She told me this was exactly the sort of prank her dead husband would have enjoyed playing!

- **Natural Events.** Sometimes the dead will give us natural phenomena that they think we will appreciate. A breeze on our cheek and nowhere else, or perhaps the sun breaking through clouds at an ideal moment and shining rays seemingly upon us alone, might be a sign from a dead loved one. Rainbows as funerals are ending or at interment services are a surprisingly common sign.

The dead work hard to give us these signs, so pay attention, especially in the first year after a death. And whenever you notice something that might be a sign, always say aloud a warm "Thank you!" and send a mental hug.

Chapter Three

Electricity, Scents, Sounds, Thoughts

"As a man who has devoted his whole life to the most clear headed science, to the study of matter, I can tell you as a result of my research about atoms this much: There is no matter as such. All matter originates and exists only by virtue of a force which brings the particles of an atom to vibration and holds this most minute solar system of the atom together. We must assume behind this force the existence of a conscious and intelligent mind. This mind is the matrix of all matter."

—Max Planck, winner of the 1918
Nobel Prize in Physics

"In quantum mechanics all particles can also be described as waves. And waves have an unusual property: an infinite number of them can exist in the same location."

—Physicist Carlo Rovelli

"I want to know how God created this world. I am not interested in this or that phenomenon, in the spectrum of this or that element. I want to know His thoughts; the rest are details."

—Albert Einstein, winner of the 1922
Nobel Prize in Physics

"The Spirit gives life; the flesh counts for nothing."

—Jesus (JN 6:63)

S ome of the signs the dead give us are subjective, happening within our minds. Many of them, though, will happen right out there in our shared reality, where anyone near us would experience them. Dead communicators have explained how each of these kinds of signs is produced, but still—as you will see— some of them are boggling from our perspective. Even having been told how they are accomplished, you will find it hard to believe they are possible.

ELECTRICAL MANIPULATION

You can imagine the joy in heaven when we started to electrify our homes! Since our beloved dead are energy beings, messing with electricity is easy for them. They can cause lights to flicker, turn televisions off and on, and even sometimes put messages on computer screens. They can extinguish streetlights as we pass beneath them, activate cellphones and answering machines, and even (rarely) dial us up for a chat.

For radios, TVs, and music boxes to turn on at a critical moment and deliver information or play songs is a surprisingly common sign from the dead. Music boxes owned by a dead loved one that have lain unused or even broken for years will spontaneously turn on as the family returns from the funeral, for example. A friend of mine had been given a music box that played the giver's favorite song. It had long been silent in a china cabinet, but then one morning, five years almost to the day after the giver's death, my friend walked into her living room and that music box spontaneously began to play "When You Wish Upon a Star."

Sometimes the electronics in a particular home will be uniquely useful to the newly-dead. I know of one widow who often finds a missed call on her answering machine that purportedly was made from the telephone attached to it. The only evidence of this impossible call is the name of her dead husband appearing as the caller.

Some of what the dead do with electricity will annoy us. They can easily burn out electric motors, and one young man who had hated the sound of vacuum cleaners in life quickly burned out four of them after his death. They might use their electrical skills to give us signs that are meaningful to us alone, such as stopping an old wall clock at a significant time or burning out letters on a neon sign so when we pass the sign its remaining letters will give us a personal message.

My brother-in-law, Jerry, died in his fifties. He was a loving man in life, and in death he is a powerful being. Almost immediately after he died, he was blinking lights and turning television sets off and on, to the point where his family had to beg him to stop messing with their favorite shows. He gave us a number of other signs that I will mention in their appropriate categories, and then about ten years after his death he gave me the most astonishing set of electrical signs that I have heard described.

Jerry's widow had moved after his death to a home that had one defective kitchen spotlight, the middle light of a group of three. I visit my sister frequently, and about ten years after Jerry's death, we found that now—amazingly—that middle light was turning on, but only if I flipped the switch. I could stand there and flip it, and it would go on each time; Jerry's widow could then flip it, and it would stay dark. And so it went for months. The fact that the light always turned on for me, but never turned on for the woman whose home it was, gave us astonishing and irrefutable evidence that there was an intelligence behind these events.

So then I pushed it. One evening I said, "Jerry, if this really is you, please this time when I turn the lights on, make the middle light stay off." I flipped the switch, and the middle light began to turn on with the others, but then it faded and went dark. I turned them off and asked that this time he turn on all three lights, and when I flipped the switch again all three lights came on and remained on. Case closed.

Although she could see that Jerry's selectively turning on her middle kitchen light this way made for a spectacular post-death sign, his widow began to feel slighted by him. And he seemed to be sensitive to that. She told me that one day she had been complaining to a friend by phone about this situation, and when she had then gone to turn on the kitchen lights, just that one time the center light had turned on for her.

Jerry's light-signs to me continued through several week-long visits, and his widow's irritation increased to the point where they were nearly having posthumous marital issues. Then, midway through one of my visits, the middle light didn't illuminate on two occasions when I flipped the switch. Mostly, though, it still worked. One evening toward the end of that week, I went into the kitchen and turned on the lights, wondering whether that center light would work for me this time. Indeed, it began to turn on with the others . . . but then it faded and went dark. I sighed, but as I turned away, the room went bright. The middle light had come back on! That was Jerry's swan song. In an apparent effort to placate his widow, no matter how many times I flipped that switch, the middle light never worked for me again.

At first this series of events was amusing—lots of thanking of Jerry, lots of joking about it—but then when he continued to operate that light only for me over months of time, it began to feel astounding. And the odds against chance for such an amazing series of selective operations of a usually disabled light are nearly incalculable.

SCENTS

People who are no longer in bodies are able to impose thoughts and impressions on the minds of living people in remarkable ways. One thing that is easy for them to do soon after their deaths is to give us whiffs of scents that are going to make us think of them. Jerry had been a smoker. The first time after his death that I visited his widow, I was setting my suitcase on the guestroom bed when I was overwhelmed by the scent of cigarette smoke. These scent signs happen in our minds, so the smoke-smell soon disappeared and I never smelled it there again.

My grandmother wore a distinctive perfume, something like lilacs and lilies of the valley. She died when I was fourteen, and often in the year after she died I would catch that precise scent unexpectedly. It was only decades later that I first understood that those whiffs had been post-death hugs from her.

Scent-signs can include anything from flowers and perfume through less glamorous things like cooking, machine oil, smoke, and soap. They tend to be delivered only in the year or two after someone's death, so that is when you should be most alert for them. If you catch a sudden whiff of anything that reminds you of your dead loved one, just speak your thanks for it and smile. A scent sign is a wonderful hug.

SOUNDS

Familiar sounds can also be impressed upon our minds, but they seem to be less common than scents. Every animal we have loved is waiting for us, now young and healthy, and those that we have especially loved will sometimes give us an unexpected familiar bark or meow. Occasionally, the bereaved will hear a dead loved one's footsteps or other familiar sounds. Widows will hear a husband working in the garage or shaving in the bathroom, and when they go and check, there is no one there. One widow reported hearing her recently-deceased husband going through his whole morning routine and then leaving the house as if heading off to work.

Producing these sounds in our minds seems to be as easy for the dead as is the production of familiar scents, but of course we find them more disturbing since they might indicate the presence of an intruder. My hunch is that is why they are relatively rare. Familiar songs, though, are another matter.

SONGS

Here is something firmly in the category of *I cannot believe they can pull this off!* But they can. And they often do. Turning on a car radio or stepping into a store or an elevator and hearing the song that you danced to at your wedding, or the song that the two of you called your special song, or a song whose refrain is the answer to a question that you have just asked your dead loved one is an astoundingly common sign. This can happen to you repeatedly, even if the song is very old or seldom heard, and it can even happen when the radio station does not ordinarily play that kind of music. Of course, one instance in the course of a day of hearing a familiar song could be chalked up to coincidence. But if the song is rare, and if you hear it several times soon after a death, then that is not random. How on earth do they do it?

Although familiar songs are a surprisingly common sign, and the dead assure us that sharing them with us is not a difficult trick, the process is somewhat complicated. The key to its success is the fact that *time* operates so differently there.

You will meet my dead friend, Mikey Morgan, when we talk about pendulum communication. Mikey has made sending songs to his family one of his specialties, and his mother says that they still come almost daily, even eight years after his death.

Here is Mikey's own explanation of how he does it:

1. I change my vibration to draw close to them in the earthly dimension.

2. I am tuned in to their plans for the day, what they are talking about, their feelings and concerns.

3. Remember we are in a timeless mode. We are not under the restraints of time.

4. We can put thoughts in your head to leave at a certain time for an event or work. Or we can put a thought in your head to go to a certain store at a certain time. We can also influence you to get distracted so you leave a little later to get the timing right in your dimension. Sometimes, when we know the song is about to play, we will channel in a memory of us, so your mind is thinking about your loved one right before the song occurs.

Okay, we're almost there. Here is how it actually happens, according to Mikey:

> We can figure out when a certain song is going to play on a radio channel or over a PA system by technology. We can also manipulate the frequencies to alter the song being played depending on if it is programmed (he means that there is no DJ). If you are listening to a different channel on the radio, but we are aware the song we want you to hear is on another channel, we will put the thought into your head to change the channel. More often, we try to manipulate you to be at the right place at the right time. Because we are in a timeless dimension, we can do some manipulating for songs to fall into place at the perfect time, if that makes sense. Radio

shows with a DJ are more challenging, but it can be done. We can put thoughts into the DJ's mind to play a song or say a certain thing. Pay attention to what songs play in a store while you are there. It might really amaze you. These songs are programmed and can be dealt with by us! The message in the song may be the answer you have been looking for with a question. Or they can be letting you know they are watching over you. Great communication can occur!

Mikey Morgan is an unusual guy. He has made it his mission to assist in revealing these truths to the world, so not only is he good at communication, but he has stayed tight with his mother even many years after his death. But songs seem to be a kind of post-death specialty. I know of other dead loved ones who are still sending song-signs long after their deaths. Whenever you hear a song that reminds you of your dead loved one, be sure to say aloud, "Hello and thank you!" Offer encouragement, and you might enjoy years of familiar songs delivered by your loved one as a post-death hobby that the two of you can enjoy together.

THOUGHTS AND VOICES

As Mikey's explanation of song-signs indicates, the dead can be in such close contact with our minds that they can impress their thoughts on us. They seem not to give us complicated thoughts, but rather their influence over our minds is more like impressing impulses: they will give us a scent or sound, or they will inspire us to turn on a radio or to look at something as part of their process of delivering a sign to us.

Our dead loved ones can also impress others to do things or to say things, and surprisingly often they will impress on the minds of others the impulse to give us what are actually gifts from them.

For example, another of Mikey's specialties is green dragonflies. He once impressed a stranger wearing a green dragonfly pin to walk up to his mother at a party. His mother admired the pin, and the guest said, "I'm going to give it to you. You need to have it." So Carol accepted without protest a pin that she knew was actually a gift from her son.

Mikey has retained his sense of humor. Recently his family was on a road trip and talking about how happy they all were and how much they needed this vacation. The radio DJ then blurted, "He likes it! Hey Mikey!" Unbelievable. I defy anyone to say that for one specific DJ to spontaneously spout a line from a thirty-five-year-old cereal commercial at precisely the right moment, and for the Morgans to be listening, was a coincidence. And the glorious thing about this family's careful acknowledgement of each of Mikey's signs is that their beloved son and brother remains such a vibrant part of their lives.

This contact that the minds of the dead have with our minds isn't creepy, and you shouldn't worry about it. They are respectful of our privacy. They want us to go on and live the rest of our lives without their interference, so their connections with our minds generally seem to be limited to just what is necessary to reassure us that they are fine.

Sometimes the dead will make us hear voices in our minds. A mother might hear a child say, "I love you, Mommy." A widower might hear his wife call him to dinner. A grieving lover might hear familiar sweet nothings. Since producing their voices in our minds is a relatively easy post-death skill, I am surprised that it isn't more commonly reported, but perhaps it is too easy for us to dismiss such voices as wish-fulfilling imagination. A sound or a scent, on the other hand, is more likely to be accepted by us as a genuine sign.

Chapter Four

Coincidences, Synchronicities, Numbers, Dreams

"The really amazing thing is not that life on Earth is balanced on a knife-edge, but that the entire universe is balanced on a knife-edge, and would be total chaos if any of the natural 'constants' were off even slightly."

—Dr. Paul Davies, Professor of Theoretical Physics

"Every interpretation of quantum mechanics involves consciousness."

—Mathematician Euan Squires

"The field is the sole governor of the particle."

—Albert Einstein, winner of the 1922 Nobel Prize in Physics

"It is evident that when many coincide in their testimony (where no previous concert can have taken place), the probability resulting from this concurrence does not rest on the supposed veracity of each considered separately, but on the improbability of such an agreement taking place by chance. For though in such a case each of the witnesses should be considered as unworthy of credit, and even much more likely to speak falsehood than truth, still the chances would be infinite against their all agreeing in the same falsehood."

—Richard Whately, nineteenth-century Church of Ireland Archbishop of Dublin, quoted by Sir Robert Barrett in *Deathbed Visions* (1926)

F or ages, those wishing to deny that these sorts of experiences were signs from the dead have been insisting that they were mere coincidences. An honest mathematician will tell you there is nothing "mere" about coincidences; and in fact, sometimes a remarkable coincidence will all by itself be a post-death sign.

COINCIDENCES

Coincidences happen in our lives so frequently that we seldom give them much thought. A friend will pop into our mind, and the next instant the phone will ring. We will board a plane and find ourselves sitting next to someone who either needs information we have, has information that we need, or knows someone that we know. We might idly pick up a newspaper or magazine and learn something crucial. We might hurry out to buy something we need and find that the store has just one left.

And sometimes, out of the blue, odd things will happen. Years ago, I randomly spotted a Borders bookstore and had a sudden, inexplicable urge to go in and buy a copy of *A Course in Miracles*. I knew about the book, but the notion of buying it had never occurred to me. I found a whole empty shelf in the spiritual section of that store that held one copy of the book, facing outward, which seemed to be odd and too convenient. **Then when the cashier tried to check me out, he told me the book didn't exist in the store's computer.** (This is the sort of thing that our spirit guides will do when they want to influence us. I bought the book and found a study group, and I began at last to do the *Course*.)

Most signs that we receive from the dead are subjective, unexpected, and subtle. Many of them would seem to be easy to explain as coincidences. Please note, though, that the odds against a certain significant thing happening at a given moment actually are pretty long. Whenever a strange thing happens, the possibility that it might be a sign from a dead loved one should be in your mind.

Coincidental signs happen so often in close association with recent deaths that even when you are in deepest grief, it's important that you pay attention. I will give you two examples from my mother's death.

- **Lilies.** My father was much older than my mother. She had promised him that he would die at home, and would leave the house that he had built for her only "feet first, with a lily in your hand." And so it was. As he lay dying, she found an out-of-season calla lily through a sympathetic florist. Since he died twenty-odd years before she did, I had forgotten my mother's promise to my father . . . until flowers began to arrive from friends who were just learning of her death. **The first that arrived were two-dozen calla lilies!** And as they were fading, another friend sent me a peace-lily plant that blooms to this day.
- **Cards.** A number of the sympathy cards that we received also seemed to be signs from my mother. I could almost see her hovering in card stores as friends and relatives made their selections. My mother had a favorite bird and a favorite flower, so I found a striking sign from her in a card I received from someone who never had known her. It was an oddly out-of-season drawing of a chickadee perched among blooming lilacs.

Whenever you receive what seem to be coincidental signs, it's important to check with those providing them. I did that. Neither of the women who had sent lilies had known about my mother's promise to my father, and the one who had sent the chickadee card was nonplussed and delighted to have been used that way.

SYNCHRONICITIES

Whether you believe in your spirit guides or not, each of us has friends not now in bodies whose job it is to assist us with our spiritual growth (even if that means they need to materialize a book they want us to read *right now* on the shelf of a Borders bookstore that doesn't carry the book in its computer, and then prod us to turn off the road as we drive by).

Sometimes our spirit guides will nudge us with a whole series of what seem to be coincidences, some subtle and some jarring, that together add up to one enormous realization that what is happening could not be random. *Synchronicities are coincidences on steroids.*

For example, you might be trying to make a decision about whether to move from Portland to Austin in order to take an offered job. Then over the course of a day, you might see the cover of an old copy of *Time* magazine with the state of Texas on it; you might spot two Texas license plates on the road; you might overhear a conversation about Austin in the supermarket; and you might notice that a house you are driving past on a road that you don't normally take is flying the Lone Star flag. Any one of those events means nothing. Even two or three might conceivably be random. But people whose spirit guides use synchronicities will sometimes report as many as ten or fifteen such events surrounding guidance they believe they are being given, and the odds against chance for so many synchronicities together are nearly incalculable.

As with every other sign that you think you might be receiving from a loved one or a spirit guide, be sure to say "Thank you!" aloud at each instance of a suspected synchronicity. I know someone who says, "I'm not convinced—I need one more," each time he suspects a synchronicity is happening. Quite often he will get his one more!

NUMBERS

Significant numbers on digital clocks, license plates, billboards, or coins, or significant numbers anywhere at all, can be important signs from dead loved ones or from spirit guides. Sometimes the numbers will be a birthday, an anniversary, or a death date. Sometimes they will be a series of the same number, with 11:11 on a digital clock said to be the most common numbers sign.

The dead can give us clock-signs, but I have a hunch that seeing all the same numbers on a digital clock is most often reassurance from spirit guides. When I am fretting about something, I might be tugged to see a series of repeated clock numbers at the top of my computer screen several times a day. There was one day when I was wrestling with a difficult project, and I saw 4:44 both early in the morning and late in the afternoon. On that same afternoon I also saw 3:33 and 5:55. I randomly glanced up to notice each of these numbers. I never looked at the clock otherwise.

You can't catch a series of the same clock numbers on your own initiative. I know that because I have tried it repeatedly. But yet, you might unthinkingly glance at a clock, and there the numbers are. There are 1,440 minutes in a day, and among them there are twelve all-same-number digital clock moments. The odds against randomly seeing even one of them in a twenty-four-hour period are long. And the odds against randomly seeing them once or twice several days a week, and week after week, are so long as to be nearly beyond calculation. As with all suspected signs, thank your dead loved ones and your spirit guides aloud and take these signs as the spiritual hugs that they are.

COMMERCIAL SIGNS, BUMPER STICKERS, LICENSE PLATES

To be thinking of a dead loved one, and at the same time to see a license plate or bumper sticker with his name or a word or phrase that reminds you of him, really brings you up short! Yet it happens all the time. Or some of the dead will prompt the bereaved to look at a commercial sign or a billboard that similarly provides part of a private conversation.

My dead friend, Mikey Morgan, has given me insights into how these signs are delivered. Bumper stickers and license plates are among his specialties, and he tells us that the fact that our dead loved ones exist out of time is essential to their delivery of these signs. To quote him:

Timing is very critical for these types of signs. We (in the afterlife dimensions) need to be aware of what is coming and going in your dimension with travel on the road. We then need to coordinate you to cross paths so you see the sign we are trying to give as you are driving. We (in the afterlife) will put a thought to you to make you aware of the license plate or commercial sign that has a message that you are about to come across as you are traveling. We can make another vehicle slow down or block a vehicle until you get close enough to see it on the back of a car. Timing is the key, but being in a timeless dimension, again, gives the advantage for us to get the job done!

COMMUNICATION DREAMS

The minds of our dead loved ones can become so closely aligned with our minds that they can give us extraordinary dreams. Dreaming about the dead is common, but communication dreams are something else, and it's pretty easy to tell the difference.

Typically, communication dreams feel like big events:

- **They are memorable.** Most dreams will fade by lunchtime. A communication dream, on the other hand, remains fresh in your memory for decades.
- **They usually involve normal-seeming physics.** In most communication dreams, the scenery looks normal and people walk and talk believably. This isn't always the case—I flew in one communication dream—but there generally is a sense of reality that isn't present in most dreams.
- **Our loved ones look and act normal.** In some communication dreams our loved ones will look as they did when they were last with us, while in others they will look much younger, but they always look like themselves. Occasionally other dead loved ones will join them, perhaps sitting around a familiar table or strolling in a beautiful park.
- **They often communicate a message.** In some dreams the message may be spoken, while in some it may involve actions that we observe or take part in. But there often is a reason for the communication dream beyond simply affirming the fact of their survival.

A few communication dreams are dark or frightening. Nearly all signs from the dead are comforting and uplifting, but I have heard about a few of what seemed to have been communication dreams that were horrid. In one, a grandmother stood in an empty room with a terrified look on her face, seemingly asking for help that the survivor had no way to give; in another, the dead loved one was wandering in a gray fog, and without awareness of the dreamer trying desperately to get his attention. People whose transitions to the afterlife are incomplete seem to be unable to communicate with us, and we know that the afterlife levels where most of the dead reside are light and happy, so I have no way to explain these dreams. Please know, however, that if you suffer a sad communication dream of a dead loved one, since there is no objective time, whatever pain he or she is presently feeling is likely to seem brief and transitory to the sufferer.

My most extraordinary communication dream was a message from my horse. I had owned him from the age of six months until he died when he was nearly thirty, and the fact that I could not be there when he was given his fatal shot was weighing heavily on my mind. Then, five nights after his death, I had an extraordinary dream that is still vivid even many years later.

There was Beau in harness in front of me, pulling the cart in which he and I had enjoyed exploring the dirt roads near our home. He was trotting along happily—he loved carriage-driving!—and I was in rapture. The only problem with driving a horse is the bugs in your teeth because you can't stop grinning. Then we had, one after another, three encounters with diesel eighteen-wheelers that had no business being on wilderness roads. Each time, as the truck bore down on us, I steered Beau into the roadside bushes and fast jumped out of the cart to hug his head against my chest so he wouldn't bolt as the truck roared past us. As the third truck—perhaps his death—was approaching, I woke up.

That had been a communication dream, but what had it meant? In minutes, I knew. We had moved twice during his lifetime, and Beau was thanking me that unlike nearly all the horses on earth, he had been kept safe during both of the moves of his life and gently cared for until he died. After that dream, I have decided that I won't ride or drive a horse again until my friend and I are reunited and I can have bugs in my teeth forevermore.

Post-death signs are so varied and so universal that it isn't much of a stretch to surmise that nearly everyone who has completed the transition to the afterlife levels leaving loved ones behind will attempt to deliver some sort of sign. Many of the dead will make repeated and varied attempts. Now that you know about the kinds of post-death signs the dead are most likely to give us, I hope you will be quick to acknowledge anything that seems even remotely to be a sign from your recently-departed loved one. If the dead think they are getting through to us, they often explore giving us more kinds of signs. When you give those you love repeated encouragement, they are likely to keep on trying until they have given you a sign or two that even a skeptical soul like yourself cannot deny!

Chapter Five

Light, Visions, and Manifestations

"The only reason for time is so that everything doesn't happen at once."

— Albert Einstein, winner of the 1922
Nobel Prize in Physics

"In my father's house are many rooms; if it were not so, I would have told you. I am going there to prepare a place for you. And if I go and prepare a place for you, I will come back and take you to be with me that you also may be where I am."

— Jesus (JN 14:2-4)

"Thomas Jefferson still survives."

— The last words of John Adams

"Oh wow! Oh wow! Oh wow!"

— The last words of Steve Jobs

ntil now, most of the signs we have discussed were subtle. Coins and birds and feathers and scents, songs and insect-clouds and digital clocks: to be frank, it is possible for even experienced researchers who receive such signs to feel unsure about whether that is what they are. But there is a class of physical signs so extraordinary, so beyond-belief wonderful, that no one who has experienced such signs can have any doubt that the dead survive.

SPIRITUAL LIGHT

Since the dead are energy beings, when they lower their vibratory rate close to ours, we sometimes can see them as light:

1.   **Spiritual Mist.** During the death process, a newly-released loved one may look to survivors like a lightly glowing mist appearing above the body and sometimes lingering briefly before seeming to dissipate. Occasionally, these mists will persist for days in a room where someone has died.

2.   **Glowing Bodies.** Rarely, someone at a bedside will see the mist rising from a dying loved one condense into a softly glowing human form still attached to the body by a glowing cord. This spirit-body may persist for a while, usually face-down above the body and parallel to it, or else sitting cross-legged in the air.

3.   **Glowing Orbs.** The dead will sometimes appear to us as orbs, even many years after their deaths. These orbs—essentially, globes of light—generally are detectable only by digital camera. I speak publicly about these subjects, and a few years back I was giving a lecture and kind of stumbling around at first. Then suddenly, it felt as if it all kicked in and the words began to flow. Someone

who had been in the audience and taking pictures with an iPhone later showed me a series of pictures taken at the start of my lecture. In one of them, a giant globe of light was obvious beside my head. Orbs generally are perfectly smooth, but this one oddly had a mouth-shaped irregularity close against my ear.

4. **Columns of Light.** Since the advent of digital cameras, we have been better able to detect dead people who have lowered their vibratory rate to match ours. My indefatigable brother-in-law, Jerry, produced a wonderful spirit photo soon after his death. His many siblings will take a group photo whenever any of them has a birthday, and in their first siblings' photo after Jerry's death there was a man-sized column of light in the back row. It couldn't have been a defect in the photo. It even shed light on the dark woodwork around it.

VISIONS

For people in grief to see visions of dead loved ones is common. The fact that most people aren't aware that the dead routinely appear to the living astounds me, frankly, since these visions of the dead can be as spectacular and life-transforming as near-death experiences and they are a much more usual experience. Post-death visions of the dead can take a number of forms:

1. **Shared Deathbed Visions.** People approaching a planned death will find dead loved ones at their bedsides, now young and healthy. This seems to be a universal part of the death process. The deceased friends, relatives, and pets that we are most likely to trust will come to us in the days or hours before our deaths to

comfort and reassure us, and then to escort us to the higher-frequency levels of reality as soon as we are free of our bodies. **The last words of Steve Jobs, who repeated "Oh wow!" three times, speak for themselves.** Raymond A. Moody, Jr. first popularized near-death experiences in his epochal 1975 book, *Life After Life*; and thirty-five years later he did the same thing for shared deathbed visions. As he documents in his wonderful 2010 book, *Glimpses of Eternity*, sometimes people sitting at a deathbed will share in these deathbed visions of loved ones. They will see the dead folks who have come to escort the person who is dying, and occasionally they will accompany that newly-dead loved one on the first part of his journey.

2.   **Visions Very Soon After a Death.** Sometimes a person who is spiritually close to someone dying far away will see a smiling vision of the person who has just died. Nearly always, these visions soon after a death will be just torso-high and silent, although they glow and appear to be very happy. Thomas Jefferson and John Adams both died on the Fourth of July, 1826, Jefferson in the morning and Adams in the afternoon. **That a moribund Adams stirred and mumbled "Thomas Jefferson still survives" shortly before his own death is an oddity with an obvious explanation.** And it cements for me the certainty that those two lifelong friends had by the time of their deaths entirely healed their political rifts!

3.   **Visions in the Year Following a Death.** Many people will see a vision of a departed loved one within the first year after the death. By some estimates, the instance of this form of communication between spouses approaches

fifty percent. Most of these communications are simply nonspeaking visions of the departed loved one looking healthy and smiling, usually appearing while the survivor is relaxed or just awakening, and often minus the lower part of the body.

4.   **Visions of Animals.** Most visits from dead pets involve familiar sounds or impressions on bedclothes, or fixed attention on one particular spot by a surviving pet. Full visions of pets are fairly rare, but recently I heard a lovely one described. "A week or two after my dog died, I heard what sounded like a dog acting up. I went to look, and there, full of life, wagging her tail, was the German Shepherd we had just lost. She looked in her prime, but what struck me most was that she was covered with thousands of tiny clear lights, as if she had frost covering her. As I watched, she faded away." That frost of spiritual light is an astonishing detail. When beings at higher levels reduce their vibratory rate so they can appear to us, typically they glow with light

5.   **Physical Materializations** I have seen reports of recently-dead loved ones turning up for a physical visit. These materializations generally happen in the family home—often, oddly, in the kitchen—and the visitors tend to look just as they did in life. Materializations are solid. If their bodies are touched, they feel warm and normal. Often they will initiate hugs. If they speak, most of what they say is just that they are fine and all is well. Materializing this way seems to require a tremendous amount of energy, so such visits typically last only minutes. *But they leave an indelible impression!*

COMMUNICATIONS FROM SPIRIT GUIDES

The afterlife evidence strongly suggests that all of us have spirit guides assisting us throughout our lives. These folks are something like ground controllers. They have lived in physical bodies, so they know the terrain; and from where they are now, they have a better perspective on our situation so they can give us what amounts to subconscious coaching.

We are seldom aware of our spirit guides' efforts because they tend not to speak to us in words. Instead, they might materialize a book for us in an unsuspecting Borders bookstore, or they cause synchronicities to pop up around us. Or they might simply plant ideas in our minds. We can have what feels like a spontaneous thought or breakthrough, or feel an inexplicable reluctance to do something, and that sort of thing could be a nudge from a guide. We can easily ignore our guides' coaching since what they do is subtle, but it doesn't pay to ignore such wonderful help from people who have dedicated themselves to helping us throughout our lifetimes.

Rarely, a spirit guide might choose to appear to us as a material being. Someone may come up to us at a meeting or be seated on a park bench or even appear at our own front door, and calmly give us advice. Since this stranger looks normal and seems friendly and non-threatening, we will listen patiently, and we might be mildly surprised at the insights given. Then when the person says goodbye, we will be very surprised indeed when we glance away and then look back and find that, impossibly, the friendly stranger has vanished into thin air. I have no idea how often this happens, but I have heard enough such stories to feel the need to mention the possibility.

Experiences of light seem to be most often visits from our spirit guides. Appendix IV contains a longer description of my two experiences of light, without which it never would have entered my mind to do afterlife research. Briefly, when I was eight years old, a young male voice spoke to me from a flash of white light saying, "You wouldn't know what it is to have me unless you knew what it is to be without me. I will never leave you again." Twelve years later, the same voice spoke from a second flash of light to remind me that, "I will never leave you." I am confident the speaker was my spirit guide, but who knows? What I do know is that these experiences are as vivid a half-century later as they were at the time, and they did what I assume they were meant to do. They shaped my life.

Experiences of light are rare, but I have heard a few others described. They seem to happen when we are in spiritual distress, and often they will prompt us to take action. At least two experiences of light are described in the Bible. Moses heard a voice speak from a bush that burned but was not consumed, and the Apostle Paul was converted from persecutor to supporter of the earliest Christians when Jesus spoke to him from out of a brilliant light.

VISITS FROM BEINGS OF LIGHT

The signs described elsewhere in this book seem nearly always to come from our recently-dead loved ones, or from our spirit guides. But there is a distinct kind of spectacular visitor that is almost certainly an upper-level being.

The more spiritually advanced a disembodied being is, the more it glows. Spiritually advanced orbs tend to be larger and brighter. When extremely advanced beings choose to appear to people on earth, they look like tall, thin, androgynous but vaguely male or female beings that glow in broad daylight. Typically they glow with a color, most often yellow or golden, but I haven't heard enough of these beings described to be able to say those are the only possible colors. The writings of all religions are replete with such visitations. Often in Scripture these visitors are called "angels," although I don't think it is possible to say for certain what they are. For our purposes, it doesn't much matter.

Tall, thin, glowing beings always seem to have something to say. Our loved ones will appear to us briefly, but seldom talk; our spirit guides usually won't appear, but sometimes we can hear them speak; these glowing folks, though, will appear spectacularly and deliver a message that matters to them.

Visits from beings of light are rare. I likely wouldn't have included them here, except that my mother received such a visit without having any idea of what it was. If it happened to her, then it must happen to others who are similarly unaware.

At the age of eighty-eight, my mother nearly died of heart failure. She came so close to death that as her coma lifted, she described to me the welcoming visits from her dead parents that she had spurned in favor of living on a while longer. I had never heard of anyone actually refusing to leave with deathbed visitors, but the significance of Mom's survival wasn't clear to me until a few weeks later. I visited her one morning in the nursing home where she was doing rehab, and she greeted me with a cheerful, "They're letting me stay longer."

"Who's letting you—?"

"They."

"'They'? How do you know?"

"The tall man told me."

She said that on the previous evening, a very tall, thin man who radiated golden light had walked into her room and said to her, "We've decided that since you want to stay, we're going to let you stay a little longer." Then he had calmly turned and walked out. Nobody else on that busy floor saw him, but I have no doubt that visit was real because my mother described a being of light in detail. She had never before known that they existed, and she had no idea what she had seen. Our glowing friend turned out to be as good as his word. Despite the fact that her doctors had told us that survival in her condition was impossible, my mother stayed in her body for another five years.

All these signs and communications, no matter what their source, require that the minds of those giving them be in very close contact with our minds. The thought of another mind so strongly influencing yours may make you uneasy at first, but I hope you will become comfortable with it. True, our thoughts are not as private as we once believed they were. But the tradeoff is this glorious loving connection with eternal Mind, and the sweet certainty that each of us and everyone we love is living an eternal life.

How We Can Communicate with the Dead

Chapter Six

Mediums

"It has occurred to me lately—I must confess with some shock at first to my scientific sensibilities—that both questions (the origin of consciousness in humans and the origin of life from non-living matter) might be brought into some degree of congruence. This is with the assumption that mind, rather than emerging as a late outgrowth in the evolution of life, has existed always as the matrix, the source and condition of physical reality—that stuff of which physical reality is composed is mind-stuff."

—Biologist George Wald, winner of the 1967
Nobel Prize in Physiology or Medicine

"A life-giving factor lies at the center of the whole machinery and design of the world."

—Physicist John Wheeler

"If you wish to upset the law that all crows are black, you must not seek to show that no crows are, it is enough if you prove the single crow to be white."

—William James, nineteenth-century Harvard
Professor of Psychology and Philosophy

61

When most people think of getting in touch with the dead, they think of consulting a medium. As you will see, there are other forms of contacting the dead now in use that don't require a medium as an intermediary, and some of them have the potential to be developed to the point where for anyone any longer to deny that the dead survive will be impossible. But for now, consulting a medium is likely to be the method of communication that is most available to you.

So, how does it work?

Contacting a dead loved one through a medium is more difficult than just phoning someone up. Nearly all working mediums now are psychic or spiritual mediums. They can be in contact with your mind and either directly or indirectly in contact with the mind of your dead loved one, but they cannot put your minds into direct contact with one another so a lot can get lost in translation. And the different types of mediums actually work quite differently.

SPIRITUAL AND PSYCHIC MEDIUMS

I confess to being skeptical of most modern mental mediums. While I was deep in doing afterlife research, I commissioned sittings with perhaps a dozen well-recommended spiritual and psychic mediums, and there were only a few who seemed to be in communication with my dead loved ones. The two who were good were very good! But some of the others did surprisingly poorly, given their reputations.

I realize now that their failures could have been my fault. I had no recently-dead loved ones who were likely to be hanging around; I knew that everyone was fine, so I didn't really need a reading; and I had come to these mediums predisposed to be skeptical. In retrospect, too, I have to say that my loved ones who showed up got thinner as my series of test-readings progressed. By the fourth or fifth, it was generally just my brother-in-law and maybe a pet. The others apparently had gotten bored and given up. No wonder some of these well-recommended spiritual and psychic mediums got poor results, and a few slipped into cold-reading in desperation.

Cold-reading is a method by which some less honorable mediums will lead us to slip them information, and they will seize on it as if it had come from the dead. For example:

Medium: "There is a woman here, older, could be your grandmother, she has a younger woman—or no—it's a man . . ."

You: "My grandmothers are both still alive. But my grandfather just died!"

Medium: "That's it! He says he's your grandfather."

Some cold-readers become so good at it that they can make a whole career as a medium, even though their mediumistic powers are so thin that most of what they share is imaginary. People who consult them are so eager to believe that they will sit through an hour of generalities and hear just two or three things that resonate, and those are the things they will remember.

All of that being said, there are some very talented and highly accurate mental mediums working today. The wonderful Gary Schwartz of the University of Arizona conducted double- and triple-blind tests of some volunteer mental mediums in which the medium and the sitter were not identified to one another and they never saw one another during the reading, and in which the sitter was allowed to say just yes or no . . . or was required to say nothing. He documented this work in his excellent 2002 book, *The Afterlife Experiments,* which made me a believer. Even under such difficult conditions, some of the mediums tested in Schwartz's laboratory were graded by sitters as having been more than ninety percent accurate.

How does mental mediumship work? All our minds are undivided parts of eternal Mind, and therefore all of us— both living and dead—are to some degree able to be in contact with the minds of everyone else. As with any other natural ability, the extent of this talent varies among individuals, and most of us learn in childhood to suppress our psychic abilities. Some, though, will actively hone these skills, while others will be beacons to the dead and will find themselves being recruited to be mediums. Still, whether or not we ever cultivate our abilities, being able to be in contact telepathically seems to be part of the human design.

Readings with mental mediums can work well, even if you and the medium are thousands of miles apart. Since you understand that beyond this material reality such things as time and distance don't matter, you likely won't consider this to be surprising. Most mediums I have met actually prefer to work by phone, since they say that seeing the person for whom they are reading can be a distraction. But don't hesitate to work with a medium who is even half a world away, since there is no distance where your loved one and the medium's guides reside. The distance between you and the medium doesn't matter.

All mediums have teams of dead guides to assist them in their work. Guides who work with mental mediums are generally skilled psychics themselves, and it is likely that each team works out with the mind of the living psychic the methods that are going to work best in their case. Here are some communication methods that various mental mediums have described to me:

• **Harvesting information from the mind of the medium.** One very good but nearly unknown medium was able to get the names Oliver, Bertha, and Jerry, and also to say how each was related to me. Those are uncommon names so I was astonished, and I asked how she had done it so easily. She said that she knows people with those names, so her guides had shown her first the person she knew whose name it was and then an indication of what my relationship was to my own relative. Easy.

- **Establishing agreed-upon symbols.** If you ever have seen John Edward work, you know that for him, red roses are a symbol of love sent by a dead loved one. Some teams have many agreed-upon symbols to act as a kind of shorthand that the guides can cause to appear in the living psychic's mind.

- **Mental conversations with guides.** It can be as if the medium is on the phone with his or her guides, and standing there next to those guides is your dead loved one.

- **Direct mental communication with your dead loved one.** This seems to be the most difficult method because the medium and your loved one are strangers to one another, but apparently some guides are good at facilitating hookups between unrelated minds.

Many mental mediums seem eventually to use a combination of methods. The more a medium and a team of guides work together, the more effortless their communication becomes, and watching the progress of their partnership can be an enjoyable experience.

John Edward is one of the psychic mediums who have been proven by Gary Schwartz's methods to be genuine. Having seen him perform four times in person, I have had the fun of watching his skills develop. Perhaps a decade ago, he would point to a section of the audience and say, "I think I'm over here. I've got a female above, feels like a mother vibration or acted like a mother in life . . ." A few people would raise their hands or stand until he and his guides had further identified the communicator. I last saw him in action in 2012, by which time he was saying crisply, "Second row, the lady in white—no, the woman next to you—your mother is coming through. She passed in a car crash." Firm, detailed, and accurate.

There are many reasons why a sitting with a spiritual or psychic medium might not be effective in your case. Here are five of them, off the top of my head:

1.   **You might be harboring strong negative emotions.** Anger, bitterness, or even just grief can act as an absolute barrier to communication through a medium. This is why most professional mediums won't do a reading for you until many months after your loved one's death.

2.   **You might have trouble believing that communication is possible.** I have said this before, but it bears repeating: open-minded skepticism is fine, but a hostile refusal to believe is an active barrier to communicating with the dead. This is a four-way partnership—you, your loved one, the medium, and the medium's guides—and for you to resist and not let it happen is going to mean that it isn't going to happen.

3.   **The medium might be having a bad day.** All professionals have "off" moments when they are ill, tired, or not in the mood. For mediums, being not quite right can shut down their ability to work effectively.

4.   **Your loved one may not want to communicate.** There is so much to do in the afterlife levels that once they have assured us of their survival, sometimes our loved ones just want to have fun. Or they may have some personal reason to avoid the connection. Although many mediums over the years had described my father accurately, he had always refused to speak. It was not until twenty years after his death that he came to my daughter when she consulted a medium, and he asked that she convey his apology to his children for having damaged their childhood. This experience taught me how important it is for us to let our dead loved ones know that we forgive them for everything! It never would have entered my mind to think that

he had harmed us in childhood, nor that he might still feel guilty about it.

5. **Your loved one may be unable to communicate.** I hesitate even to mention this possibility. It is unlikely to affect anyone you love, and I don't want you to worry about it. Very rarely someone will go offtrack in the death process, or will feel so burdened by guilt that he will consign himself to what Jesus accurately called the "outer darkness" level of post-death reality. And people who have not completed their transitions or have dropped to the punishment level seem to be beyond the reach of mediumistic communication. Ideally, we will forestall such problems while we are alive by (a) learning more about the actual death process, and (b) making sure that we have forgiven others and ourselves as much as possible before we die.

Why might a spiritual or psychic medium get something wrong? With most mental mediums, the process is something like a children's game of "telephone." Your loved one conveys something mentally to the guides; they then relay it mentally to the medium; then the medium tries to interpret it accurately, and finally conveys it to you. We can't be sure about that first step— between your loved one and the medium's guides—but most communication on the afterlife levels is telepathic, and for their purposes it works well. But their perspective is very different from ours, and things can get lost in translation. Mental mediums tell me that the worst times are when a dead person uses an absolutely spot-on piece of shorthand that the living sitter is sure to recognize, but the medium doesn't realize that is what is going on.

For example, the image that comes to the medium from his guides might be a wildcat crouching on a rock. So he might say, "Oh, so your dad says that you and he used to hunt together?" You say, "No! He hated guns!" Then it turns out after some red-faced confusion that your shared favorite sports team is the Bobcats. The symbol mistakenly interpreted to mean hunting might as easily have been an actual gun, with the eventual revelation that your father's proudest fact was that he had been a Marine. Most mental mediums and their guides soon learn to convey exactly the words and symbols they are given, and they let the sitter figure out what they mean.

The best spiritual and psychic mediums are very good indeed! Please be sure to check references, though, and remember that even a very good medium might not be successful in your case.

DEEP-TRANCE MEDIUMS

The late nineteenth and early twentieth century was the heyday of deep-trance mediums. Only a handful are working now, so there is little point to our saying much about them, but you ought to know something about their glory days. **If the best evidence of human survival that was received through deep-trance mediums a hundred years ago had not been suppressed and ignored, you would have lived your whole life knowing that it never is going to end.** That is how good the deep-trance method is at delivering evidential information, and how hard dead scientists were working at the time to give us effective proof of their survival.

What appears to be needed for talented living psychics to develop as deep-trance mediums is many years of sitting in the dark night after night, concentrating on mediumistic communication. In the days before radio, in America and England, people from the more prosperous classes often got together for dinner. Afterward the men would retire to smoke, and the women might sit around a table in a darkened room, indulging in the fad of table-tipping. Everyone would put their hands on a table. A question would be asked. Then the table would begin to lift and tap, spelling out the answers letter by letter. The method used generally involved having the table tap enough times to get to the position of each new letter in the alphabet, so this took a while!

Generally when table-tipping worked very well there would be found to be one or two people at the table who were talented psychics. And as all those evenings of sitting in the dark piled up, month by month and year by year, some of those psychics developed their abilities to levels that perhaps have not been seen since. Eventually, a few of them became such extraordinary mediums that they learned to withdraw from their bodies altogether and let their primary spirit guide—often called their "control"—speak directly using the medium's vocal cords.

This elimination of one of the steps in what we think of as the mediumistic process—your loved one to the medium's guides to the medium to you—made a world of difference in message clarity. As researchers began to study these mediums, fascinating books soon appeared that contained verbatim transcripts of conversations between a grieving relative and a deep-trance medium's control that were highly evidential. Instead of relying on the mind of the medium to make sense of transmitted words and symbols, the control would spout detailed and often chatty comments received directly from the dead relative. I recall reading about one sitting with a deep-trance medium in which a man who had died in old age rather bitterly railed against family members who had put things right on top of his will in the bottom left drawer of his dresser, so of course now nobody could find it! The lost will was found where the man had said it would be found.

My favorite early-twentieth-century deep-trance medium is Gladys Osborne Leonard. Her work was studied extensively by Charles Drayton Thomas, a Methodist minister, and her primary control was a woman named Feda who had died hundreds of years before. As word got out that a tremendous amount of evidentiary material was being produced through deep-trance mediums, the scientific community naturally rushed to protest that the mediums were just reading the minds of dead relatives in the room. This time, rather than giving up, the dead researchers working with Leonard began to deliver what were called book tests, a method of proving their existence that they thought that even professional debunkers never could find a way to refute.

In one form of book test, Feda would give Thomas an address and a location within a house, and would describe a certain book on a designated bookshelf. She would predict that on a specified page and line of that book, certain words could be read. Thomas would record Feda's prediction and post it to the British Society for Psychical Research before he went and begged the indulgence of those living at that address so he could check out Feda's prediction. He said at the time that the dead were right in their book-test predictions more than ninety percent of the time, and he thought that what might be recorded as their misses were actually his own mistakes. We have no idea how the dead were able to read closed books, but they did it over and over again. When volumes detailing various kinds of book tests began to hit shelves, rather than opening their minds, the scientists of the day ignored them altogether.

Appendix II lists as resources three books by Charles Drayton Thomas that detail some of his work with Gladys Osborne Leonard and Feda. I found Thomas's books to be fun to read, but reading them in order gives you a sad sense of opportunity lost as you watch Thomas transform from a careful and professional researcher to a man discouraged by all that scientific hostility and only going through the motions.

PHYSICAL MEDIUMS

Like deep-trance mediums, physical mediums are very rare today. They are also especially talented mediums with skills developed to an extraordinary degree, but their gifts are different in that they are able to manipulate our reality. They might bring forth random noises or voices; emit a material called ectoplasm, which can be used to build hands or bodies for conjured spirits; or facilitate any number of extraordinary effects. And all of this might be happening while the medium is locked in a cabinet, mouth taped and hands bound, behind a curtain and in a trance besides. The best physical mediums working today are able to facilitate meetings with dead loved ones who materialize in the room and can talk with us, can touch and even hug us. The impact of such a meeting on someone living with grief can be life-transforming.

The minds of our dead loved ones remain intimately connected with our own minds. Despite the fact that they are on a different, higher-frequency channel, they are as close to us as the air we breathe.

Chapter Seven

Ancient Methods

"Astronomy leads us to a unique event, a universe which was created out of nothing and delicately balanced to provide exactly the conditions required to support life. In the absence of an absurdly-improbable accident, the observations of modern science seem to suggest an underlying, one might say, supernatural plan."

— Arno Penzias, winner of the 1978
Nobel Prize in Physics

"Neither the religious nor the scientific (person) can longer afford to ignore the facts presented here, to pass them by."

—Frederick W. H. Myers, nineteenth-century
skeptic and later afterlife researcher

"History shows that every intelligent man who has gone into this investigation, if he gave it adequate examination at all, has come out believing in spirits; this circumstance places the burden of proof on the shoulders of the skeptic."

—James H. Hyslop, nineteenth-century
skeptic and later afterlife researcher

"Well if I am not Hodgson, he never lived."

—Richard Hodgson, nineteenth-century
debunker and later afterlife researcher,
communicating after his death

*T*here are a few ways in which the living can attempt to communicate with the dead that don't fit any category. All these methods have ancient roots, and all of them are still in use, but for various reasons they seem to be out of the running where the search for a consistent and dependable means of communicating with the dead is concerned. Let's briefly examine four of them.

OUIJA BOARDS

Since the advent of the "talking board" in the 1890s, people have over and over discovered and rediscovered Ouija boards. Simply put, an Ouija board is a flat surface with numbers and letters arranged on it and a smoothly moving planchette on which two or more people place their fingers. A question is asked, and the planchette moves as if by magic to spell out an answer. By the 1950s, Ouija boards were toys. I recall having one as a child.

My opinion of Ouija boards is simple. Never use one. Ouija boards might summon family members, but they can just as easily serve as beacons to call in nasties who will then be happy to wreck your life. The evidence is strong that some of the most bitterly negative people may choose not to complete the transition to the afterlife levels. While most of these dudes have little power, some have power enough to do us harm. Healthy adults have a natural energetic defense system, but the very young, the very old, and those who are spiritually weakened can easily be attacked by these beings.

The history of Ouija boards is replete with tales of people inadvertently summoning groups of negative entities who proceeded to make the user's home their own. Sometimes persuading these unpleasant beings to leave turns out to be impossible. Occasionally, a home must be abandoned. Don't attempt to use a Ouija board when there are safer and more effective ways to communicate with your beloved dead.

AUTOMATIC WRITING

Some of us have a latent ability to allow the dead to write using our hands poised with pen and paper or at a keyboard. Even people who are not otherwise psychic might discover that they can do automatic writing, and the more they do it, the better their abilities become.

I know how you feel. For decades, I had trouble believing in automatic writing. How do we know that automatic writing isn't just the deluded or fraudulent meanderings of the sitter's own mind? Here is how we know:

1. **The handwriting is consistently different.** Faking a different handwriting that is internally consistent and then keeping that up over pages of rapidly scrawled work is impossible, to be blunt. It's impossible. Try it.

2. **The handwriting often matches known examples of the communicator's handwriting.** Sometimes this is how people who are just discovering that they have this ability will recognize their communicators: they see that distinctive handwriting.

3. **It often happens rapidly.** Time being different where the dead reside, and the vibratory rate there being more rapid, once a communicator has confident control of his scribe, the writing can happen so rapidly that an assistant has to keep supplying new sheets or the writing goes off paper altogether.

4. **Material received this way can be consistent in every detail with what is received by other means.** Some of our best and most detailed summary accounts of what the afterlife levels are like have been received by means of automatic writing. In all such cases of which I am aware, the sitter had little prior afterlife knowledge, but from that naïve hand flowed information known

only to people who had spent decades studying the afterlife evidence.

So now I read material received by means of automatic writing with an open mind, but I still don't attempt to do automatic writing. Here is why:

- **An automatic writer can be a beacon for negative entities.** The dead describe the situation precisely that way: someone sitting poised and ready to write whatever a spirit wants to write will cause spirits to home in as if on a beacon. The evidence is overwhelming that very bad actors who have shed their bodies do exist, so although negative possession is less commonly reported with automatic writing than with Ouija boards, to offer to give voice to random discarnate beings is potentially dangerous.
- **Automatic Writing is a Serious Commitment.** If you find that you can give expression to beings who are not in a body and you want to spend the time needed to develop this skill, then first please seek out a good psychic with experience in this area who can help you learn how to protect yourself. I don't have the time to devote to learning how to do it; automatic writing simply is not my voyage. If you think it may be your voyage, just please be careful!

SCRYING

Scrying is a general term applicable to several methods of making contact with the dead. In all cases, a shiny or reflective surface backed by something opaque enables entities not in this material dimension to be seen. Crystal balls work this way. Mirror-gazing, involving black-backed mirrors, does as well. Even a broad bowl filled with water (or, anciently, blood) can be used. The indefatigable Raymond Moody has done extensive and fairly successful work in replicating the ancient Greek Oracle of the Dead at Ephyra, and his 1994 book, *Reunions,* is a must-read for anyone interested in this field. For most of us, however, scrying is not going to be an especially effective method of communication.

PENDULUMS

There was a recent time when pendulums seemed to me to be the worst way to try to communicate. It would be easy for someone to fake the swinging of a pendulum, and the whole thing looked so clumsy that I couldn't believe any self-respecting dead person would use a pendulum when there were better alternatives. *But then I met Mikey.*

In the spring of 2011, I attended a conference on the afterlife where I met Carol Morgan, a woman who had lost her twenty-year-old son a few years before. Carol clearly was out of her depth. She knew nothing about the afterlife, and talking with people who were knowledgeable in this field made her tongue-tied. She stumblingly told me that she had learned how to communicate with her son via pendulum, and if I had the time she would love to show me how this pendulum thing worked. I wouldn't have joined her in her room for a demonstration if she hadn't seemed so touchingly clueless. I couldn't bear to hurt the feelings of a woman still grieving for her child.

That afternoon, I made two new friends. Carol sat down with a crystal pendulum on a string that was suspended over a flat disc of letters and numbers laid on a table, and she called for Mikey. The pendulum began to move. Carol was transformed. She and Mikey were soon chatting and laughing (something Mikey did by wildly swinging the pendulum), and all the while her arm and hand holding the pendulum never moved. As I studied her from all angles—got my nose right down there next to her—Mikey brought messages of love and comfort to three grieving mothers in the room. He was still a fun-loving twenty-year-old. "Hey, your daughter's really cute!" he told a woman who had just lost a teenager. Mikey's messages were acknowledged as evidentiary by all three mothers as, one by one, he brought them to tears.

But what got me about this experience was Carol. A woman who had seemed insecure and tentative was chatting animatedly with her son, full of love and delight and barely acknowledging that the rest of us were there. No one on earth is that good an actress!

Since that day, I have watched Mikey Morgan answer hundreds of afterlife-related questions. Carol remains clueless about these matters, to the point where sometimes she apologizes when she finds what Mikey says to be unbelievable. But she needn't worry. In all this time and through hundreds of thoughtful and detailed and sometimes esoteric answers, I have never seen Mikey make a mistake.

There is no doubt in my mind that Mikey Morgan is exactly what he claims to be. He is a being who has achieved the level of spiritual development just below the Source, and who chose an additional brief life and an early death so he could re-accustom himself to life on earth and then communicate through Carol to help us better understand what really is going on. If you would like to hear more of what a playful twenty-year-old who lives on what he calls the teaching level of the afterlife has to say, you should know that Mikey Morgan has written a terrific book called *Flying High in Spirit—A Young Snowboarder's Account of His Ride Through Heaven.*

So . . . now I can see that pendulum communication can be the right choice for even sophisticated entities. It isn't for everyone. But when a being no longer in a body needs to communicate with the help of someone who is not especially psychic, using a pendulum might work well.

Still, all of these more esoteric methods of communication seem to be out of the running where the present search for a reliable broad-scale method of contacting the dead is concerned. **Let's talk now about some modern areas where researchers are achieving wonderful results.**

Chapter Eight

Induced Communications

"When I began my career as a cosmologist some twenty years ago, I was a convinced atheist. I never in my wildest dreams imagined that one day I would be writing a book purporting to show that the central claims of Judeo-Christian theology are in fact true, that these claims are straightforward deductions of the laws of physics as we now understand them. I have been forced into these conclusions by the inexorable logic of my own special branch of physics."

—Frank Tipler,
Professor of Mathematical Physics

"We have before us one sole aim . . . we come to demonstrate to man that he is immortal, by virtue of possession of that soul which is a spark struck off from Deity itself."

—Imperator, quoted by William Stainton
Moses in *Spirit Teachings* (1883)

"We are not human beings on a spiritual journey. We are spiritual beings on a human journey."

—Pierre Theilhard de Chardin,
French Philosopher and Jesuit Priest

"I shall be with you always, to the very end of the age."

—Jesus (MT 28:20)

One fruitful area of current research into developing better methods of communicating with the dead is what is called induced communications. I have spoken with people who have experienced induced communications, and I can testify that those I spoke with were thrilled by the experience. All claimed to have had highly evidentiary encounters with their dead loved ones that reduced their grief substantially.

Induced communications apparently happen inside the grieving person's mind. Since you understand now that all our minds are part of one universal Mind, and you realize that our minds and the minds of the dead are separated only by their different rates of energy vibration, it won't surprise you to learn that methods are being developed to connect our minds directly. And some of what experts in this field are achieving is extraordinary.

COMMUNICATIONS INDUCED BY THERAPISTS

A few licensed therapists are pioneering methods by which their grieving patients can have personal encounters with dead loved ones that immediately and substantially reduce their grief. The quiet and delightful Rochelle Wright is one such therapist. Her procedure uses bilateral stimulation, in which the left and right sides of the brain are stimulated alternately. Wright prefers to use two senses to accomplish this bilateral stimulation of the brain: she plays music that alternates in volume between the left and right speakers of a set of headphones, and she also prompts the experiencer to rhythmically move his or her eyes in what Wright says is a mimic of what happens in deep REM sleep.

After a short period of this bilateral stimulation of the brain, experiencers are told to close their eyes. For most of them, a wonderful meeting with a dead loved one begins to unfold. When it ends, experiencers open their eyes and tell the therapist what they have experienced, and then the bilateral stimulation process is repeated and another experience is encouraged to develop in a session that can go on for hours.

Wright reports that in 95% of the sessions she has conducted, her procedures have induced life-changing connections with dead loved ones that in some cases have nearly eradicated what had been overwhelming grief. Many of these experiences are amazingly vivid, happening on beaches or on mountain trails and including long conversations and real physical hugs. Wright has taught more than forty licensed psychotherapists to use her procedures, and they are now being used successfully all over the United States.

SELF-INDUCED COMMUNICATIONS

R. Craig Hogan is a relentless pursuer of some method — any method — that will bring the fact that our lives are eternal into broader public awareness. His knowledge of the afterlife evidence is extensive, and his 2008 book, *Your Eternal Self*, is an easily-understood classic. Hogan has helped some fellow researchers write about their own discoveries, and in doing that he came upon the whole area of therapist-induced communication with the dead. Soon he was pioneering a way for individuals to learn to make their own contacts with dead loved ones in the comfort of their homes.

Hogan's Self-guided Afterlife Connections procedure uses relaxation activities with guided meditations presented in eight training stages. At each stage, participants learn to become more adept at allowing experiences to unfold naturally in their subconscious minds until awareness of loved ones now in spirit begins to dawn and they can share what are often intense experiences. Those who are open to Hogan's techniques and devotedly follow them can get to a point where they can sit alone anywhere and directly connect with loved ones now living in the afterlife. Many experiencers report absolutely real and genuine encounters that happen in beautiful places. Some experiencers even say with amazement that eventually their dead loved ones will be physically present in the room.

R. Craig Hogan is a man on a mission. His method of learning to do self-guided afterlife connections is available to you for free at http://selfguided.spiritualunderstanding.org.

Although these techniques have been amazingly successful, you can immediately see a problem. What—this all happens in your mind? Then how do we know you aren't imagining it, or even making it up? Having spent time with some experiencers, I am confident that they aren't faking it. But like all the other methods of contacting the dead that are personal and subjective, it is difficult to use these methods to convince skeptics that we survive our deaths. **The next method, though, eventually is going to be used to do just that.**

Chapter Nine

Electronics

"Everyone who is seriously involved in the pursuit of science becomes convinced that a spirit is manifest in the laws of the Universe - a spirit vastly superior to that of man, and one in the face of which we with our modest powers must feel humble."

—Albert Einstein, winner of the 1922
Nobel Prize in Physics

"If you equate the probability of the birth of a bacteria cell to chance assembly of its atoms, eternity will not suffice to produce one . . . Faced with the enormous sum of lucky draws behind the success of the evolutionary game, one may legitimately wonder to what extent this success is actually written into the fabric of the universe."

—Organic Chemist Christian De Duve,
winner of the 1974 Nobel Prize
in Physiology or Medicine

"The spirit-world is around you though you see it not . . . the spirit-world extends around and about you, and interpenetrates what you call space."

—Imperator, quoted by William Stainton
Moses in *Spirit Teachings* (1883)

"For whatever is hidden is meant to be disclosed, and whatever is concealed is meant to be brought out into the open. If anyone has ears to hear, let him hear."

—Jesus (MK 4:22-23).

I nstrumental Transcommunication (ITC) includes Electronic Voice Phenomena (EVP). This field seems to be the most promising area of evidential afterlife communication. Not only are dead researchers and their living collaborators learning to employ these techniques with ever more skill and sensitivity, but some of them are working now to come up with what has been called the holy grail of afterlife communication. They seem to be closer to developing some version of a telephone by which we can call up dead Aunt Martha and have a chat with her.

RESEARCH TEAMS

For anyone doing original research in afterlife communication, having a good team of dead collaborators is essential. In this field, most of the work is done by the dead and not by the living, so living researchers are the laboratory assistants of people whose knowledge in this field is much greater than their own. Evidence strongly suggests that dead researchers have been seeking trustworthy living collaborators for decades, and the delay in achieving reliable methods of two-way communication may have less to do with what is possible than it has to do with the fact that so few of the living have been able to invest the extensive time and dedication that was necessary. Whenever breakthroughs were achieved, those moments were fleeting as daily life pulled away the living collaborators.

EARLY EXPERIMENTERS

Most people who hear the terms ITC and EVP think immediately of television shows in which researchers go ghost-hunting in dimly-lit places with primitive recording equipment. What they generally produce is what sounds to me like background noise and static. I have never been impressed, and I imagine that you have learned long since to write off the very idea of communicating with the dead electronically. So you will be relieved to learn that, out of the spotlight, living researchers working with teams of dead experts have been achieving wonderful results in electronic communication for more than thirty years.

The modern recording of ITC and EVP had a hopeful beginning in the seventies and eighties, when adventurous living researchers, most notably Americans George Meek, Sarah Estep, and Mark Macy together with a number of remarkable Europeans, were working with dead research teams that included prominent people who in life had been interested in proving human survival of death. The communications produced by just these teams alone are so astonishing and so evidentiary that if the mainstream scientific community had been sufficiently open-minded to study their recordings and the methods by which they were produced, you would have known for decades that human minds are eternal. Here are a few of the things that early researchers were able to do effectively:

- **Communication with the dead via radios, televisions, and various "black box" devices.** Many of these methods have been proven to produce evidentiary information—voices, pictures, sometimes even conversations—but for various reasons none of them seems to be a likely candidate for an efficient method of two-way, real-time communication.

- **Communication with the dead via their telephone calls** is another means by which teams of dead researchers have been giving us evidence of their survival since at least the mid-eighties. The dead who have used this exciting alternative have told us that they generally build a telephone at their own frequency level of reality directly over the target phone that exists on this level of reality, and then they place a call. The earth-level phone rings. When it is answered, people who are known to be dead are heard speaking, using voices and mannerisms that are recognized by those who knew them in life. When the phone bill later is received, there is no record of the call.

• **Communication with the dead via their putting material on computers** has been happening randomly ever since personal computers first were used. There are a number of well-documented instances of researchers finding on computers that were not connected to the Internet clear pictures, letters, and other kinds of communication that dead researchers claimed to have produced.

Unfortunately, the scientific community either ignored these early researchers' work or tried to debunk it. Eventually most prominent living researchers either died or lost heart. Association TransCommunication, founded by Sarah Estep in 1982, still patiently documents communications from the dead that are being received electronically by its members, and meanwhile individuals all over the world continue to work beneath the radar with their teams of dead researchers. The scientific stonewalling of this amazing information continues, but that may be about to change.

THOSE NOW WORKING IN THIS FIELD

Since roughly the turn of the present century, fresh teams of dead experimenters are beginning to take another stab at bringing the truth of their survival to humankind. This time, their intention seems to be not so much to convince the living researchers working with them that electronic communication with the dead can happen. That milestone has long since been reached. But rather, there are indications now that they are working to develop methods of electronic communication that are so clear and so reliable that for the mainstream scientific community to continue to stonewall these truths will be impossible.

All the early methods listed above involved receptive living researchers who were working with and taking the lead from experimenting dead researchers. These attempts must be seen as just the testing of alternatives, an effort on the part of the dead to build methods that eventually will allow the living to initiate contact whenever we like. And at last, that stage is being reached. The method that currently shows the greatest promise for ease of use by the living involves computers, and it requires a living facilitator and a team of dead researchers who are expert at working together. Hearing a dead child say, "Mommy! I can speak!" or a mother offer reassurance to her son in her own distinctive voice is an unforgettable experience.

Verified conversations initiated by the living and facilitated through computers have been recorded between not just recently-dead loved ones and their survivors, but also comatose individuals and those who care for them. The current state of development of this method makes real-time conversations difficult, since the living person generally asks questions or makes comments and then pauses before speaking again, and once the call is ended and its recording is replayed, the words of the dead or comatose communicator are found to have been appropriately inserted. Or alternatively, sometimes the dead person's answer is found to have been recorded before the question was asked. These technical difficulties may be caused in part by the difference in concepts of time, but I don't think anyone yet knows why they happen.

We have lately learned one important reason why developing reliable two-way communication with the dead has been such a difficult process. In the spring of 2015, teams of dead researchers announced to their living collaborators that there are low-level entities in the way, at the vibratory level of the outer darkness, who long have been working to block communication. Clearing out these nasties is the responsibility of the dead researchers, and they say now that it will take a few more years but that their efforts will be successful. Learning what has been wrong is half of solving the problem. The day when you will be able to ring up dead Aunt Martha and ask for her recipe just recently came a little closer!

Telegraphic communication may be easier to achieve at first than computer communication. There are teams working on various methods of using pulses of energy or light controlled by the dead to deliver messages and pictures to the living.

IT WON'T BE LONG NOW

When it comes to establishing a reliable and on-demand means of communicating with the dead, proof of concept has been established. You might say that we are a good three decades past the Wright Brothers' first flight. And a number of things are different now from what they ever have been before:

- **We have many clear and authenticated recorded communications from people known to be dead.** Those researchers on both levels of reality who were working thirty years ago may have been ignored by their contemporaries, but their work laid an important foundation.
- **Old belief systems are losing their hold on our culture.** This seems to be a necessary step for us to open our minds to what the dead are saying, and it is happening now with astonishing speed. All over the world, religions are either declining or feeling forced to resort to totalitarianism in order to remain relevant. Yet many surveys indicate that people in general are becoming more spiritual. The field of our beliefs is being cleared for fresh seeding.
- **Mainstream science is declining in our esteem.** For more than a century we were enthralled by miracles bestowed

upon us by the wise and benevolent high priests of science, but for a couple of decades now there hasn't been much more forthcoming. Worse, some scientists are resorting to totalitarian means to advance their own ends. They are uttering the words "settled science," which any scientist working fifty years ago would have indignantly protested. No science can ever be seen as settled, or scientific progress becomes impossible. The response to all of this is what you would expect. People are becoming more cynical about science, and more prone to questioning scientific pronouncements. And that is a good thing.

• **Our leaders are much more often now being seen to have feet of clay.** The reason that the thin and dishonest field of debunkery has been so effective in suppressing the truth about the afterlife for so long is that until the dawn of this new century, there seems to have been a general sense—in the United States, at least—that our most trusted institutions were working for our benefit. I challenge you to find anyone who believes that any longer.

When the U.S. Congress has an approval rating in the single digits, and when science hasn't done much for us lately, it is easier for people to see debunkers for the self-serving suppressers of the truth that they are.

The afterlife communication equivalent of heavier-than-air flight is regularly happening now, which means that what we might think of as the equivalent of regular commercial flight probably is not far behind. There is a growing sense among researchers that the day is not far away when communication with the dead will be so easy that it will have become irrefutable knowledge that human minds are eternal. **This time, I think the world really will change.**

Chapter Ten

What's Next?

"... how surprising it is that the laws of nature and the initial conditions of the universe should allow for the existence of beings who could observe it. Life as we know it would be impossible if any one of several physical quantities had slightly different values."

—Steven Weinberg, winner of the 1979
Nobel Prize in Physics

"Neither was it intended that the two worlds, ours and yours, should be as they are now — so far apart in thought and contact. The day will assuredly come when our two worlds will be closely interrelated, when communication between the two will be a commonplace of life, and then the great wealth of resources of the spirit world will be open to the earth world, to draw upon for the benefit of the whole human race."

—Monsignor Robert Hugh Benson, speaking
from the spirit realm through Anthony Borgia
in *Life in the World Unseen* (1954)

"There are two ways to be fooled. One is to believe what isn't true; the other is to refuse to believe what is true."

—Philosopher Soren Kierkegaard

"If you hold to my teaching, you are really my disciples. Then you will know the truth, and the truth will set you free."

—Jesus (JN 8:31-32)

After thousands of years of artificial separation, this is the century when the living and the dead will at last join hands across dimensional boundaries. It could have happened a hundred years ago if the mainstream scientific community had been less self-protective and more curious, but bygones are bygones. As always, truth wins. Whether this new day dawns within the next few years or in the second half of this century is still to some extent dependent on how soon the scientific community gives up its efforts to suppress the evidence, but there is good reason now to hope that progress will happen sooner rather than later.

The greatest electronic breakthrough in the field of afterlife communication is not related to the afterlife at all. It is the Internet. Before vast and easily searchable databases of information became widely available to laypeople, folks with scientific credentials could call themselves "skeptics" and then engage in the dishonest tactics that debunkers of the truth have perfected. They got away with it because for centuries there was no easy way for most of us to find alternative sources of information. Happily, that is no longer the case.

It is easy now to debunk the debunkers. In this young century we enjoy the broad and unfiltered dissemination of information. When you can just Google "Electronic Voice Phenomena" and find websites containing many wonderful recordings that include the 1994 phone calls that dead researcher Konstantin Raudive made to living researchers Sarah Estep, George Meek, and Mark Macy, it is not possible any longer for debunkers to interpose themselves between you and the truth.

By now, we have sufficient sound and well-studied information about what we are, what reality is, and what actually is going on to fill a good-sized library. Because the afterlife communications have been so consistent and so detailed, we can now say with confidence what happens at and soon after death. Led by the growing public acceptance of near-death experiences, all that information derived from studying nearly two hundred years of communications from the dead is seeping into the public consciousness, at first in a trickle but now in a flood. **The truth is being exposed to more and more people who are more disposed than ever before to look at it objectively.**

Judging by how quickly these concepts are advancing in the public mind, it could take as little as a decade more before sufficient people will have learned the truth for a tipping-point to have been reached. But it could take longer. What is needed is some fresh, non-debunkable fact that people can seize upon. Once enough of us have embraced that new fact, both scientific and religious authorities will have no choice but to accept it and begin to find ways to integrate it into their paradigms. We already know that those who should have been our leaders in the search for the truth are going to be the last to acknowledge it.

It seems clear now to many researchers that our one essential bit of world-changing information is likely to be news of a workable spirit phone, or soul phone. Not a phone that can record the voices of the dead; not a way for them to give us signs of their survival; not a way for people to stay in touch: we have had these things for decades, and they have been ignored. No, what is needed is a way for anyone dealing with grief to ring up someone who has recently died and have a genuine real-time chat.

That will do it. When people all over the world are regularly turning for the assuaging of their grief to having actual conversations with a recently-dead child or spouse, then all the desperate debunkers on earth will no longer be able to turn back this tide. I think that to make progress very soon, nothing less is going to be enough. I also think that a workable soul phone may be no more than a decade away.

It won't be easy. As you know, those living in the afterlife levels are on a higher vibratory channel, and most forms of electronic contact between levels still require operators with mediumistic abilities being led by teams of dead researchers. The obstacles to a simple, reliable means of mechanical communication are nearly insurmountable, to be frank. If it were easy, it would long since have been done. But things really do seem different now.

For one thing, **living researchers have a better understanding of how reality works.** It wasn't until the early years of this century that quantum-physics-for-dummies books became widely available to non-scientists, and afterlife researchers quickly saw the similarities between quantum physics and the physics that functions in the greater reality as the dead describe it. Better understanding how physics works in the afterlife levels and how this material universe fits into a much greater reality has made it easier for living lab assistants to cooperate with dead researchers. As a result, some of the teams seem to be making real progress. For the first time, it is possible for those of us who are watching it happen to envision how direct electronic communication with the afterlife levels might work.

WHAT DIRECT COMMUNICATION WILL MEAN

Broad awareness that communication with dead people is reliably happening won't help just the dying and the newly bereaved. In fact, it will change everything. Western societies are grounded in a materialist perspective that has kept physicists in the weeds for more than a century. We Westerners might believe in a theoretical heaven, but what we know for sure is that we are separate individuals who live briefly and then die, and who had better get as many material pleasures for ourselves as we can manage before our minds blink out. What we are certain that we know is the precise opposite of what is true.

Think about that for a minute. Reality is not material, we are not separate, we live eternally, and the greatest pleasures are grounded in Mind. Everything that modern Western societies are certain about is wrong! And as each of us internalizes this beyond-wonderful new understanding of what reality is and what our minds truly are, there is nothing about the world we see around us that will remain unchanged.

We cannot say for certain how the future will then unfold, but we can guess:

1. **Most people will begin to think in terms of living eternally.** The realization that our minds cannot die is going to impact everyone's life. Based on my observations of the lives of people who already know the truth, I can tell you that more and more of us will become kinder, more loving, and more oriented toward living on an eternal scale. The negatives of this lifetime will matter less. Spiritual development will become the central pursuit of many more people's lives.

2. **Fears will lessen remarkably.** Fear of death is the base fear. As that dissipates, we can expect to see a rapid rise in freedom from fear, and with it, a concomitant joy. Knowing that everyone you love is with you forever makes you the happiest that you can be!

3. **We will want to know more.** Studying the afterlife is addictive. As ever more people realize that it is possible to know what is going on, and that it's all good, interest in learning these truths will escalate.

4. **Trust in faith-based answers will decline.** We are seeing a lessened interest in religions now all over the world. For people to learn that their faith-based institutions have been preaching things that they can see now are wrong is likely to accelerate religion's decline. Fortunately, there are religion-like organizations—the Unity Movement is one of them—that carry forward the Gospel teachings of Jesus, now further supported by

the afterlife evidence, while they abandon Christian dogmas that the afterlife evidence does not support. Similar organizations are likely to arise in other faith traditions. Perhaps "faith" will be held in less esteem, while joy in knowing the truth will come to the forefront of our relationship with Spirit.

The four points above are predictable. We can be pretty certain they will happen. But what excites me is what could come next! It is becoming possible to imagine that once we are past religious squabbling, and once most people are living in eternity and taking responsibility for their own spiritual growth, the differences we now perceive among peoples and countries and cultures could start to lose their importance in all of our minds. **We might enjoy an outbreak of peace on earth.**

This is such a thrilling time to be alive! We are privileged to help to build awareness in a weary and frustrated world that each of the more than seven billion people on earth, and uncounted billions more in the afterlife levels, is a precious part of eternal Mind. **The sooner that realization dawns, the sooner we can come together in the perfect love that is our birthright.**

Appendices

APPENDIX I

Brief Suggested Study Guide

You may find this book hard to believe until you have done some of your own research. Fortunately, afterlife-related evidence is abundant now and widely available, and if you want some personal pointers, the books suggested here are some of my favorites. Everyone who has an obsessive hobby is unable to believe that others don't share it, but you may already have your own hobbies. If you want to cut to the chase, I will first give you eight central resources. Read only these, and then go back to living your life with the glorious understanding that those who have gone ahead are fine and they always are only a thought away. Or if you find that you have more time, Appendix II is a more extensive guide where I can welcome you into sharing my passion.

Eight Key Resources

The first book given here summarizes the quantum physics that governs our greater reality in a way that non-scientists can enjoy. The second is an accurate afterlife account that was recently written by an elevated being who teaches the newly-dead how to communicate with those left behind. The third is the venerable classic in this field. And the fourth is a great summary of the current state of play in afterlife communication. All are brief and easy to understand and a lot of fun to read, so please read them first. And the four books that follow them are the absolutely stunning work of one of the world's leading experts on the greater reality and what actually is going on. If you have the time, please read these eight books, and then go on with my love to enjoy your best and most joyous possible life and afterlife!

- *Quantum Enigma* (2006) – Bruce Rosenblum and Fred Kuttner have so much fun with the physics of consciousness that they have done what I would have thought would be impossible. They have written an enjoyable physics page-turner.

- *Flying High in Spirit – A Young Snowboarder's Account of His Ride Through Heaven* (2015, 2018) – Mikey Morgan with the help of his mother, Carol, has written an extraordinary and easily understood summary of his own afterlife experiences. Mikey is a very high-level being, reportedly now upper sixth level, who had last lived on earth in the 1600s. He wanted to be able to communicate with you and me in modern terms, so he took a twenty-year additional earth-lifetime that ended in 2007. Now he communicates through his mother by pendulum, and he teaches people who are newly arrived in the afterlife how to send their families signs of their survival. Everything he tells us is amply corroborated by other communicators. For someone so spiritually advanced to be communicating with us in the 21st century as a modern American kid makes his book important, and it is a cheerful delight to read!

- *Hello From Heaven!* (1995)—Bill Guggenheim and Judy Guggenheim wrote the pioneering book on signs and visitations from the dead. The Guggenheims interviewed some 2,000 people and collected and categorized more than 3,300 accounts of their experiences. This book has become a classic.

- *Afterlife Communication* (2014)—Expert presenters at the 38th Annual Conference of The Academy for Spiritual and Consciousness Studies have here assembled chapters on the state of play concerning sixteen proven methods of afterlife communication and eighty-five accounts of extraordinary communications facilitated by these methods. Despite the bounty of information this book contains, it is an easy and enjoyable read.

Dr. R. Craig Hogan is among the world's leading experts on the greater reality. He has lately produced four books that together provide a college-level course on the afterlife and what actually is going on. These books are so terrific that they ought to be on everyone's reading list!

- *Your Eternal Self: Science Discovers the Afterlife* (2021) - This is the updated and expanded second edition of Dr. Hogan's 2008 breakthrough treatise about what actually is going on. Your mind is *not* produced by or contained in your brain. And your mind is an individual expression of the Universal Intelligence of which we all are a part —we really are all one Mind!
- *Reasons for What Happens to You in Your Life and Your Afterlife: Revealed by Speakers in the Afterlife* (2021) - Dr. Hogan uses information from residents of the life after this life to help to explain what happens to each of us through all the major stages of life: deciding to enter Earth School; planning the Earth School experience; learning to succeed in Earth School; growing in love, compassion, and understanding; graduating; and living in the life after the Earth School life.
- *There Is Nothing but Mind and Experiences* (2021) – Here Dr. Hogan explains that the Universal Intelligence is the basis of reality, and we are all individual expressions of it. He explains how we know this is true, and what it means for your life.
- *Answers to Life's Enduring Questions: Given by Science Discoveries and Afterlife Revelations* (2021) – This is an easy-to-read summary of the contents of the other three books. It is meant primarily for people who want the information but not the detailed explanations and evidence.

These eight works will give you some of the best current information about what makes eternal life possible, what the afterlife is like, how our loved ones communicate with us, and how to make the most of this lifetime so you can have your best eternal life. Perhaps that will be enough. If it is, just let me add that if you ever have questions, you can contact me at *www.RobertaGrimes.com* and I will do what I can to find your answers.

APPENDIX II

References List

You may be able to perfectly and joyously inhabit the eternal life that is your birthright only after you have done some of your own research! To aid you in that process, here are more than seventy books on seventeen primary topics that I have found to be useful as we work to better understand what actually is going on.

I. Things Are Not What They Seem

Given the depth and range of the afterlife-related evidence now available, it is a sorry fact that the mainstream scientific community continues to ignore it, and even tries to debunk it. This scientific stonewalling is millennia old, although its more active phase seems to have begun at the start of the twentieth century, just as the pioneering quantum physicists were proving that things are not what they seem. Fortunately, dedicated folks have been studying the evidence on their own, so this lack of curiosity on the part of mainstream scientists is little more than an inconvenience.

- *A Lawyer Presents the Evidence for the Afterlife* (2013) - Victor Zammit and Wendy Zammit have spent decades gathering and presenting afterlife evidence to anyone who will listen. If you are having trouble accepting the fact that there even is an afterlife, here is where you might begin your education.
- *Your Eternal Self: Science Discovers the Afterlife* (2021) - R. Craig Hogan gives us an updated and expanded second edition of his 2008 breakthrough treatise about what actually is going on. Your mind is *not* produced by or contained in your brain. And your mind is an individual expression of the Universal Intelligence of which we all are a part —we really are all one Mind!
- *Reasons for What Happens to You in Your Life and Your Afterlife: Revealed by Speakers in the Afterlife* (2021) - R. Craig Hogan uses information from residents of the life after this life to help to explain what happens to each of us through the major stages of life: deciding to enter Earth School; planning the Earth School experience; learning to succeed in Earth School; growing in love, compassion, and understanding; graduating; and living in the life after the Earth School life.
- *There Is Nothing but Mind and Experiences* (2021) - R. Craig Hogan here explains that the Universal Intelligence is the basis

of reality, and we are all individual expressions of it. He explains how we know that this is true, and what it means for your life on earth.

- *Answers to Life's Enduring Questions: From Science Discoveries and Afterlife Revelations* (2021) - R. Craig Hogan here gives us an easy-to-read summary of the contents of his other three books that were issued in 2021. This fourth volume is meant primarily for people who want the perspectives but not the detailed explanations and evidence.
- *The Biology of Belief* (2005) - Bruce Lipton is a cell biologist who got off the mainstream science reservation and never looked back. Like Hogan's book, Lipton's is so fundamental that it should be one of the first things you read as you get your feet wet in doing wider research. Lipton also recorded a CD set called The Wisdom of Your Cells that makes a great companion to his book.
- *Is There Life After Death?* - Elisabeth Kubler-Ross was a physician who specialized in death and dying, and this CD story of her personal journey – told in her wonderfully-accented voice – is compelling. If you don't make the time to listen to Kubler-Ross, your life will forever be the poorer for it.
- *The Secret Life of Plants* (1972) - Half a century ago, Peter Tompkins and Christopher Bird wrote such an extraordinary book that I am amazed that so few people have heard of it. It is a long book and not directly on point, but if you have the time, please read it. I read this book when it was first published, and even today I wince a little when I cut a tomato or grate a carrot.

II. Consciousness as the Source of Reality

The conclusion that consciousness is the source of reality will come to you only gradually, as you read more and more death-related evidence and you realize there is no other explanation. If you want to speed up the process, here are ten very different books, four of them by physicists, which should get you there more quickly.

- ***Quantum Enigma*** (2006) - Bruce Rosenblum and Fred Kuttner are adventurous academic physicists, and here they give us an enjoyable summary of their understanding of the consciousness issue in quantum physics. This book is plainly written and highly accessible for non-physicists, so it gives you a great place to begin your physics studies.
- ***The Idea of the World*** (2019); ***Why Materialism is Baloney*** (2014) - Bernardo Kastrup is a brilliant young Dutch scientist who has written a half-dozen scholarly but very accessible books that point to the non-material nature of reality. Here are the two that are most relevant to our research.
- ***The Self-Aware Universe*** (1995) - Amit Goswami is a physicist who understands many of the implications of quantum theory. His book is a little tough for non-physicists, and because it takes into account only Eastern religious teachings, it can be a struggle for the rest of us to grasp. Still, it is fascinating support for the fundamental truth that Consciousness (or Mind) is all there is.
- ***The Physics of Consciousness*** (2000) - Evan Harris Walker was another physicist. He is said to have been the founder of the modern science of consciousness research, and although he tries to simplify the physics, his book can be a tough slog in spots. Still, I loved every mind-bending minute of it. Walker died in August of 2006. After more than fifty years apart, he is again with Merilyn, the love of his life, who died when they were both sixteen, and (his dedication says) "without whom there would be nothing."
- ***My Big TOE*** (2007) - Thomas Campbell is a physicist whose consciousness theory of everything is entirely consistent with what afterlife researchers have learned independently. I first

met Dr. Campbell soon after this book was published, and I was astounded to see how close his theory of everything based in traditional physics was to the one that I had developed using the afterlife evidence. What wonderful validation! His book is meant for physicists, so it is another hard slog for laypeople. But it is altogether worth the effort.

- *The Unobstructed Universe* (1940) - Stewart Edward White worked in the 1930s. You will be astonished to find that more than seventy-five years ago he was writing about consciousness as the source of reality, the indestructibility of consciousness, and so much else! There are few books so basic. You will enjoy both him and his psychic/spirit wife, although you may find this book (if at all) only in an antique paperback.

- *Our Unseen Guest* (1920) - Darby and Joan (pseudonyms) worked with Stephen (also a pseudonym), a soldier killed in World War I, and a century ago they published a seminal account which identifies consciousness as the source of reality. The first half of their book is an insightful study of the problems inherent in communicating through mediums. The second half is the earliest reasonably accurate account of the reality revealed by the afterlife evidence that I have yet found. I feel about this book very much as I felt when I realized how completely modern evidence agrees with the teachings of Jesus in the Gospels: if they got it right so long ago, then Darby and Joan both reinforce and are reinforced by what the evidence now tells us. And when eventually some physicist is acclaimed as the mother of a consciousness theory of everything, she ought at least to acknowledge the fact that plucky young Stephen was there long before.

- *The Conscious Universe* (1997); *Entangled Minds* (2006) - Dean Radin is an academic parapsychologist whose interest lies in the workings of psychic phenomena in a quantum reality. Dubbed by some "the Einstein of consciousness research," he never quite says that everything springs from consciousness. But his books are filled with evidence of the primary role of consciousness, and they are well done and fascinating reading.

III. The Nature of Your Mind

If you have trouble grasping the fact that your brain does not generate your mind, here are some books to help you better understand what and where your mind is and how powerful it is. Like it or not, the reality you create is your own!

- *Brain Wars* (2012) - Mario Beauregard is a professor of neurology and radiology who has written an engrossing and highly readable summary of the battle now raging between scientists who are still trying to find a source of the human mind inside the brain, and those who have come to accept the fact that the human mind is separate and pre-existing. If you are having trouble making this important leap of understanding, then Beauregard's book is for you.
- *An End to Upside-Down Thinking – Dispelling the Myth That the Brain Produces Consciousness, and the Implications for Everyday Life* (2018) - Mark Gober has written a smart and highly enjoyable summary of the modern case against scientists' erroneous assumption that the brain generates consciousness.
- *The Holographic Universe* (1991) - Michael Talbot's masterwork remains a classic in this field. Much more evidence has been developed in the decades since this author published and soon thereafter died young, but his book remains one of the most important resources on this subject.
- *The Field* (2001) - Lynne McTaggart is an essential pioneer in this area. This book is indispensable background, and she also recorded two wonderful CD sets called *The Field* and *Living the Field* if you would rather listen than read.

- *The Power of Eight - Harnessing the Miraculous Energies of a Small Group to Heal Others, Your Life, and the World* (2017) - Lynne McTaggart's more recent book is a wonderful guide to using the power of our minds in practical ways to improve our lives.
- *One Mind: How Our Individual Consciousness is Part of a Greater Consciousness and Why it Matters* (2014) - Larry Dossey, MD is a scientist who follows the lead of physicists Max Planck and Albert Einstein in explaining what underlies reality in simple terms that laypeople can understand. For you to begin to internalize the true nature of your mind and the nature of God will considerably aid your efforts to grow spiritually.
- *The Divine Matrix* (2007) - Gregg Braden is another pioneer in helping us to understand where and what our minds really are, and his book is fascinating and highly readable.

IV. The Post-Death Realities

We have nearly two hundred years of abundant and consistent communications from the dead, most of the best of which were received in the late nineteenth and early twentieth centuries. The fact that there are so many communications, and they have been coming to us for so long, from different parts of the world and in a number of different ways, is not what is most significant. *What still astounds me is the fact that all these hundreds of communications describe the same complex and wonderful post-death reality!* In decades of reading afterlife communications, I have never found an outlier. I will here give you some of what afterlife experts consider to be the best summaries, together with two older channeled works that are believed by experts to be genuine.

- *Flying High in Spirit - A Young Snowboarder's Account of His Ride Through Heaven* (2015, 2018) – Mikey Morgan with the help of his mother, Carol, has written an extraordinary and easily understood summary of his own afterlife experiences. Mikey is a very high-level being, reportedly now upper sixth level, who had last lived on earth in the 1600s. He wanted to be able to communicate with you and me in modern terms, so he took a twenty-year additional earth-lifetime that ended in 2007. Now he communicates through his mother by pendulum. Everything he tells us is amply corroborated by other communicators. For someone so spiritually advanced to be communicating with us in the 21st century as a modern American kid makes his book important, and it is a cheerful delight to read!

- *The Afterlife Revealed – What Happens After We Die* (2011) - Michael Tymn is a venerable expert in the field of afterlife communication, and his brief book is a wonderfully detailed summary of what we learn from studying afterlife communications.

- *The Afterlife Unveiled* (2011) - Stafford Betty is a professor of religion, and a good friend of Michael Tymn's. Their books – both brief and easy to understand – make great companion volumes for people beginning to understand the afterlife realities.

- *The Fun of Dying – Find Out What Really Happens Next!* (2010, 2015, 2021) - Roberta Grimes wrote a brief explanation of the afterlife realities for laypeople. This book is meant specifically for those who need an easy summary of this information because they themselves are sick or because a loved one has just died, but general readers have called it an easy and happy way to begin their afterlife studies.

- *Afterlife Interrupted – Helping Stuck Souls Cross Over* (2018) - Nathan Castle is a Dominican priest who helps people who died in an accident, in battle, or otherwise at a time other than at a planned exit point, and who then were in the grasp of such severe negative emotions that they did not completely transition. Fr. Nathan helps them to complete their journeys home. The process he describes is perfectly consistent with what we know about the afterlife and the greater reality, and this wonderful book breaks some amazing new ground!

- *Life in the World Unseen* (1954) - Robert Hugh Benson was a Catholic priest who discovered after he transitioned that his book, *The Necromancers* (1907), was altogether wrong. So through his friend, Anthony Borgia, he wrote a series of books, of which this is the first and the best. In fact, many researchers consider this to be the most comprehensive and accessible account of the afterlife ever communicated to us. I urge everyone who has any interest in this field to read it, especially since it is now available for free on the Internet.
- *Testimony of Light* (2009) - Frances Banks was an Anglican nun who died in 1965, and whose account of the period soon after her death is full of beautiful and touching stories and gorgeous scenes, all consistent with the rest of the evidence.

V. The Design and Functioning of Other Realities

Our biggest problem in studying the realities that we enter at death is that we must get our information from fallible human beings. Whether they speak from beyond the veil, or, like Bob Monroe, they only visited the extra-material realities and returned, our reporters often know little more than we know, believe it or not. This means that it is important to read many after-death accounts, since the more of them we read, the more we can see that each is giving us a slightly different miniscule glimpse of what is the same gigantic set of after-death realities.

- *The Place We Call Home – Exploring the Soul's Existence After Death* (2000) - Robert J. Grant gives a brief and lucid examination of the extra-material realities based primarily on the Edgar Cayce materials. I have concerns about relying on Cayce because some of his predictions have been wrong. (Actually, my studies suggest legitimate reasons for his errors, but a treatise on Cayce is, like so much else, beyond the scope of this book.) Because Grant's book is simply written and what he reports is reasonably consistent with other sources, his book may be a good introduction.

- *Journeys Out of the Body* (1971); *Far Journeys* (1985); **Ultimate Journey** (1994) - Robert Monroe was a successful businessman with an interesting hobby. At about age 40, he learned how to leave his physical body whenever he liked and travel in extra-material realities, which afterlife researchers call the astral plane. A bright and ruthlessly honest researcher, he wrote three books that together present a gripping story of his own development. Monroe's books detail these realities from the viewpoint of someone who has not died, and therefore he was not protected in his travels as you and I will be at death. From his out-of-body perspective we see less of the scenery and more of the scaffolding. What is interesting about his books to me is the fact that nevertheless Monroe describes essentially the same beyond-material realities that we discover from other sources. His perspective lets us better appreciate how lovingly the post-death process is designed to protect and nurture our minds.

- *Cosmic Journeys* (1999) - Rosalind A. McKnight was one of Bob Monroe's Explorers, the volunteers who replicated his out-of-body work under laboratory conditions. Her book describes her experiences as a naïve and untrained but fearless participant. The first part is a bit silly, but the second half is great, and the view of astral reality that she sets forth here is amply corroborated elsewhere.

- *After We Die, What Then?* (1987); *Enjoy Your Own Funeral* (1999) - George W. Meek spent his retirement studying the after-death realities. His books are easy and enjoyable reads, and they contain useful diagrams of the upper levels and the nesting of your various bodies – so long as you always remember that all the levels and bodies exist in the same place (to the extent that talking about "place" means anything). Meek was an important Instrumental Transcommunication (ITC) and Electronic Voice Phenomena (EVP) pioneer, so his books also contain interesting sections on these topics.

- *Journey of Souls* (1994); *Destiny of Souls* (2000) - Michael Newton hypnotically regressed a number of people in deep trance to what they said were their lives between lives, and he reported in these books what they told him. After having read many tales from dead people, I was astonished to read these books and find that the accounts they contained were different from most of the others. They seemed oddly impersonal, even mechanical, although the after-death process that they described was consistent with what I had found elsewhere. It was only later that I thought about the possibility that when we are under deep hypnosis, we may be accessing our eternal subconscious (or superconscious) minds rather than the conscious minds of the individuals who have just died. If that is true, then these books are interesting for that fact alone. Most of what they say is reasonably consistent with other evidence, although they also contain some things that I have not been able to corroborate. These shouldn't be the first books on this topic that you read, but later on if you are curious and open-minded, you might enjoy them.

- *Our Unseen Guest* (1920); *The Unobstructed Universe* (1940) - Darby and Joan and Stewart Edward White were colleagues nearly a century ago, and the two books listed here are the earliest reasonably accurate modern summaries of afterlife details that I have found. The fact that I came across them only after I had pieced together most of this from other sources made them astounding to me, although if I had read them decades ago, I might not have taken them seriously. These books are highly readable, and you will find them to be both informative and still on the cutting edge. I urge you to read them, even though you will find them only in libraries or in used paperbacks.

VI. Near-Death Experiences

We are consistently told by those who are dead that death is always a one-way trip, and people who return from NDEs never actually reach the afterlife levels. This is why many accounts of their experiences are aberrant and tinged with religious symbols meant to comfort them. The primary value to the rest of us of stories told by NDE experiencers is the wonderful sense that most of them have of an all-pervading love, and the plain assurance that people's minds can function independently of their bodies. Since they are coming back, those assisting experiencers through their NDEs and back into their bodies will give them only experiences that will further their earthly spiritual growth, and will work to avoid burdening them with imagery that might confuse or trouble them.

- *Evidence of the Afterlife* (2010) - Jeffrey Long, with Paul Perry, has published what is billed as the largest study of near-death experiences ever conducted. It focuses on statistical compilations of many experiences gleaned through his website, and it also shows how common NDE details (like the fact that those blind from birth are able to see during NDEs) help to prove the reality that our minds can function apart from our bodies. Long and Perry claim that their book "reveals proof of life after death." If you need to see such proof before you venture ahead, then their book is for you.

- *Beyond the Light* (Revised Edition – 2009) - P.M.H. Atwater had three NDEs in 1977, and she spent the next four decades investigating the phenomenon. NDEs are highly variable from individual to individual, but they are consistent across cultures. The fact that infants and young children have the same experiences that adults do (except that they don't have unpleasant NDEs) helps to prove that NDEs are more than just suggestion-induced fantasies. Atwater has written more than a dozen good books, including the enormous and daunting *The Big Book of Near-Death Experiences* (2007), but this one seems to be the best for our purposes.
- *Life After Life* (1975); *The Light Beyond* (1988) - Raymond A. Moody, Jr., is the first popularizer of near-death experiences, and by now he is something of a legend. The experiences that he describes are commonly reported by people who attend a lot of deaths.
- *Ordered to Return* (originally published as *My Life After Dying*, 1991) - George G. Richie, Jr., had what may be the most elaborately detailed near-death experience ever, and his brief book is a classic in this field. Moody calls it "the best such book in print."

VII. Deathbed Visions

Less well known today than near-death experiences are deathbed visions, even though they appear to be a universal part of dying. All the books listed here are enjoyable and fascinating, and I suggest that you read at least one of them.

- *Death-Bed Visions* (1926) - Sir William Barrett wrote what remains the classic work on deathbed visions, and his brief book is a wonderful read. Unfortunately, it is long out of print and it may be hard to find. Reading it made me see how sad it is that today most dying people are so well sedated that they (and we) miss some wonderful experiences during the moments that they spend in two realities.

- *At the Hour of Death* (1977) - Karlis Osis and Erlendur Haraldsson detail a study of some 50,000 terminally ill patients observed just before their deaths by a thousand doctors and nurses in the United States and in India. Osis and Haraldsson are able to rule out medical explanations for these patients' before-death visions, and they show us that these experiences are much the same in both cultures.

- *One Last Hug Before I Go* (2000) - Carla Wills-Brandon's summary of modern deathbed visions and other before-death and at-death phenomena is a worthy successor to Sir William's pioneering volume. It was this book that helped me understand why it is that deathbed visions may be necessary. Those newly freed from their bodies are apparently so clueless and confused that without the guidance of dead loved ones and guides they can easily go off-track.

- *Glimpses of Eternity* (2010) - Raymond A. Moody, Jr. has done it again! Having coined the term "Near-Death Experience," he went on thirty-five years later to coin the term "Shared Deathbed Experience." His research indicates that some of those sitting at the bedsides of the dying will see the visions of loved ones and the next levels of reality that the dying typically see, and some even leave their bodies and join the departing spirit on the first part of its journey. As is true of everything that Raymond Moody and Paul Perry write together, this book is an easy and enjoyable read.

- *In the Light of Death* (2015) - Ineke Koedam is a Dutch researcher whose important book is a powerful contribution to the literature of deathbed experiences.

- *Words at the Threshold* (2017) - Lisa Smartt conducted a broad study of the things that dying people say in the days and weeks before they transition, and the result is a fascinating compilation which includes some phenomena that have not previously been observed.

VIII. Signs and Messages from the Dead

Those living on the afterlife levels are far more aware of us than we are of them, and naturally our grief pains them very much. It seems that millennia ago, dead people learned how to manipulate our reality with their minds so they could send us signs of their survival. By now, it seems to be an almost universal phenomenon that those who transition successfully will pause to send a few comforting post-death signs before they venture forth to enjoy the glorious afterlife realities.

- *Hello From Heaven!* (1995) - Bill Guggenheim and Judy Guggenheim wrote a voluminous book on spontaneous signs received from the dead. Often the closest survivors of those who are recently dead will experience communications of various kinds, and some of them are spectacular! Indeed, it has been estimated that more than half of widows and widowers see a vision of the departed spouse within the first year. The Guggenheims interviewed some 2,000 people and collected and categorized more than 3,300 accounts of their experiences.
- *Messages* (2011) - Bonnie McEneaney lost her husband in the World Trade Center Towers on 9/11. Soon thereafter, she began to receive signs from him, and other survivors heard from their lost loved ones as well. McEneaney collected many of these accounts into a book that also includes premonitions and messages received in other ways. This a beautiful and moving account of a group of people who left their homes one morning not expecting that they were about to die, and then

they were desperate to assure their families that they were still okay.

- *Afterlife Communication* **(2014) -** Expert presenters at the 38th Annual Conference of The Academy For Spiritual and Consciousness Studies assemble chapters on the current state of play concerning sixteen proven methods of afterlife communication and eighty-five accounts of extraordinary communications facilitated by these methods. Despite the bounty of information this book contains, it is an easy and enjoyable read.

- *The Fun of Staying in Touch* **(2014, 2016, 2021) -** Roberta Grimes presents a simple summary of the types of signs that the dead typically send to us, and also of some of the methods of communication that we can initiate with them.

- *The Survival of the Soul and its Evolution After Death* (1921, 2017) **-** Pierre Emile Cornillier was a meticulous researcher whose wonderful book containing an amazing three hundred and seventy-odd pages of séances held during the heyday of physical and deep-trance mediumship has recently been republished.

IX. Spiritual and Psychic Mediums

I still have trouble believing in the work of mental mediums. I can't get past the fact that they are mind-reading with dead people! And often the dead people whose minds mediums are reading are their own guides, which guides are in contact with our dead relatives. It all feels too tenuous to me. But that is just me. Gary Schwartz's book has convinced me that my prejudices are wrong, and I have recently come to understand that good spiritual and psychic mediums can be very good indeed.

- *The Afterlife Experiments* (2002) - Gary E. Schwartz of the University of Arizona is one of very few academically trained scientists who are investigating the afterlife evidence in a traditional university setting. Something of a skeptic himself, he uses strict scientific methods to study psychic mediums under laboratory conditions with remarkable success. For this book, he subjected some of the most prominent living mediums to double-blind and triple-blind experiments, and he found in some cases that the odds against chance for the results of their readings were in the multiple millions to one.

- *The Amazing Afterlife of Animals: Messages and Signs From Our Pets on the Other Side* (2017) - Karen A. Anderson has made a specialty of assisting bereaved pet owners by receiving for them messages from their recently departed pets.

X. Physical and Deep-Trance Mediums

The late nineteenth and early twentieth centuries were the heyday of physical and deep-trance mediums. What appears to be needed for talented living psychics to develop these skills is many years of passively sitting in the dark night after night, and in the days before radio there were folks who started with fads like table-tipping and went on to become amazingly good trance mediums. Physical mediums in trance are able to produce extraordinary phenomena and even full materializations, and deep-trance mediums can withdraw from their bodies and let a dead medium (called a control) speak, using the living medium's vocal cords. Recent efforts to resurrect both skills in Great Britain and in the United States are showing some initial promise, but the journey to full development for a talented trance medium is a long one! Meanwhile, I have given you here a recent encyclopedic compendium; two recent books about physical mediumship; two important books by a current leading afterlife researcher; a fascinating set of early accounts by a different researcher; and also three accounts of the work of an important early-twentieth-century team.

- *Great Moments of Modern Mediumship – Volume I* (2014) - Maxine Meilleur has assembled a breathtakingly complete account of the various kinds of afterlife evidence to be found in the annals of mediumship, from the mid-nineteenth century onward.

- *Unfolding Physical Mediumship: Historical, Philosophical, and Personal Perspectives* (2018) - Susan Barnes has written an excellent and easily read summary of the overall history and the current state of play in physical mediumship.

- *In Pursuit of Physical Mediumship* (2007) - Robin Foy has a long personal history in the field of modern British physical mediumship, notably including his involvement in the Scole Experimental Group. His book is a colorful journey though his personal experiences in the field.

- *The Articulate Dead – They Brought the Spirit World Alive* (2008) - Michael Tymn is a venerable expert in the field of afterlife research. This is his seminal book on the heyday of evidential afterlife communication.

- *Resurrecting Leonora Piper: How Science Discovered the Afterlife* (2013) - Michael Tymn's book about the "white crow," Leonora Piper, is a must-read.

- *Spectral Evidence I & II* (2017, 2018) - Riley Heagerty has made a career of researching and bringing to light the more obscure aspects of the heyday of spirit communication around the turn of the 20th century. His books are dead-on accurate, and they read like candy.

- *Some New Evidence For Human Survival* (1922); *Life Beyond Death With Evidence* (1928); *In the Dawn Beyond Death* (late 1930s) - Charles Drayton Thomas was a British Methodist minister who worked with a deep-trance medium named Gladys Osborne Leonard and her dead control, Feda. He was a curious and methodical fellow investigating what he saw as a cutting-edge phenomenon that was delivering world-changing information. Reading these books in order gives you a sad sense of what a lost period the whole twentieth century really was. Scientists had spent the latter part of the nineteenth century disparaging and trying to debunk all evidence related to mental telepathy and other psi phenomena. Then the early twentieth century brought a flood of afterlife communications produced through deep-trance mediums, so scientists of the day changed their tack. They began to insist that these were not communications from the dead at all, but the mediums were reading the minds of living relatives. So then some of the teams of dead collaborators who were working with deep-trance mediums set out to prove their existence to scientists by devising clever tests for themselves which would rule out the possibility of mind-reading. Thomas's 1922 book is less interesting to us than are the other two listed here because most of it is patient documentation of the results of these self-tests by the dead delivered to help scientists overcome their skepticism. The dead passed nearly all their own tests, so by the time of Thomas's 1922 book, mainstream science had changed its course again and was ignoring all phenomena that did not fit with materialism. If you have never heard of Charles Drayton Thomas and his century-year-old book of proofs that were given by his dead collaborators, you know that even then mainstream science's stonewalling was sadly effective.

XI. Automatic Writing

Some of the most interesting first-person accounts by dead people have been received by means of automatic writing. Someone with mediumistic ability sat with pen in hand or with fingers on the keys, and a dead person with similar abilities then wrote as if those hands were his own. The books listed here are quick and enjoyable reads, and nearly all of what they tell us is amply corroborated elsewhere. If you can accept how they were received, they are a useful introduction to the post-death realities.

- *Life in the World Unseen* (1954); *More About Life in the World Unseen* (1956) - Robert Hugh Benson was a British Catholic priest who died in 1914 and discovered after his death that some of what he had written during his lifetime about the afterlife was wrong. So through his friend, Anthony Borgia, he wrote these corrective manuscripts. I came across his books late in my research, and I found them to be so consistent with what I had already learned from other sources as to be frankly astonishing. No matter where these two volumes came from, they are useful first-person accounts of how the afterlife levels can appear to those who are newly arrived.

- *The Book of James* (1974) - William James and Susy Smith wrote an entertaining book that is mostly consistent with the rest of the evidence. William James, the brother of novelist Henry James, was a late-nineteenth-century Harvard professor of psychology and the first president of the American Society for Psychical Research. Susy Smith was a psychic and a prominent researcher during the 1970s, when this book was dictated.

- *Testimony of Light* (1969) - Frances Banks and Helen Greaves have given us a fascinating portrayal of Banks's early adjustments to life after death. Banks was an Episcopal nun and a spiritual seeker all her life. So many of the details of her account of what happened to her after her death are so consistent with other evidence that her slim volume is well worth reading.

XII. Guided or Induced Afterlife Connections

The afterlife evidence and insights provided by quantum physics seem more and more to suggest that everything that we consider to be real is happening in what we might begin to think of as a universal Mind of which each of our minds is a part. So it shouldn't be surprising that some of the most promising research into personal contact with the dead involves communications that seem to be happening in our minds, while at the same time they are happening in an external and palpable reality. I cannot explain this promising new field, so I'll let some of its pioneers do that for you.

- *Induced After-Death Communication: A Miraculous Therapy For Grief and Loss* (2014) - Allan L. Botkin, Raymond Moody, and R. Craig Hogan have updated and reissued a remarkable book that Botkin and Hogan first co-authored a decade ago.
- *Guided Afterlife Connections* (2011) - Rochelle Wright and R. Craig Hogan are among the pioneers of an extraordinary set of procedures that enable grieving people to meet with, talk with, laugh with, and even hold hands with and hug their dead loved ones. I have met some of the earliest experiencers and heard directly from them about meetings with the dead that seemed to be almost unbelievable. The proof was in the pudding, though: people who had been distraught with grief told me that their grief had been nearly eliminated altogether in one session. Some of them now enjoy regular visits with a dead husband or child. Amazing.
- *Reunions: Visionary Encounters With Departed Loved Ones* (1994) - Raymond A. Moody, Jr. and Paul Perry describe Moody's extensive work in the 1980s with a psychomanteum patterned on the Oracle of the Dead that was used for 2500 years at Ephyra in ancient Greece. Moody and his clients have had considerable success with this method of contacting the dead. He continues to offer the use of his psychomanteum to seekers, but he tells us that the process of preparation is extensive and "is not to be taken lightly."

XIII. ITC and EVP

Instrumental Transcommunication (ITC) and Electronic Voice Phenomena (EVP) are in their infancy, but this field of research begins to show such promise that we can now pretty well foresee that within a few decades electronic communication with the dead will likely be common. As is true of so much of what is involved in getting this information to the world, the most important ITC and EVP researchers are teams of dead scientists. The biggest barrier to advancement in this area has long been a deficit of living researchers who could act as these dead scientists' patient and very-long-term laboratory assistants. That problem seems to be ending, however, and the dead now working in this field seem to be feeling a new urgency about making breakthroughs.

- *Miracles in the Storm* (2001); *Spirit Faces* (2006) - Mark Macy has for decades been at the center of ITC and EVP research, and his books are a good introduction to these subjects. The first book listed here details how almost a decade of promising research fell apart in the late 1990s because clashes among some of the living researchers caused their dead collaborators to withdraw. The second book includes a summary of some extra-material details gleaned from Borgia's *Life in the World Unseen* as well as two similar primary sources.
- *Electronic Voices* (2010); *Glimpses of Another World* (2021) - Anabela Cardoso is a venerable Portuguese researcher working with an eminent team of the dead. She has achieved some extraordinary results.

XIV. Group Contacts

What is needed for real evidential contact to take place between our level of reality and the levels occupied by the dead is the sincere long-term commitment of living people to the process. The dead know who is genuine and who is not, and sometimes when they find a group that seems to them to be worth the effort, a team of the dead will begin what for them is a difficult process and use their living collaborators as a way to deliver validating evidence. The best ITC and EVP have been produced this way, as have been most other remarkable proofs, like apports (items materializing in air), images produced on film, and even human materializations. I have never heard of a team of dead collaborators who began the process and then tired of it, but living people seldom devote the time and energy required for more than a few years' time; and shockingly, sometimes the mischievous dead will interrupt the most successful group experiments. What happened briefly in the village of Scole in Norfolk, England, in the mid-nineties is an example of the sort of wonderful result that can be obtained by dedicated living researchers who are willing to let their dead collaborators take the lead.

- **The Scole Report** (1999) - The most extensive report to date on collaborations with the dead is available as a research paper that was printed in the Proceedings of the Society for Psychical Research, Volume 58, Part 220, in November of 1999. You can find it in many university libraries, and if you resort to copying it you will want to make color copies of its wonderful illustrations. *The Scole Report* describes a scientific investigation of some extraordinary validations that were visited on The Scole Experimental Group from 1993 through 1998 at Scole in Norfolk, England.
- **The Scole Experiment** (1999) - Grant and Jane Solomon worked with the Scole Experimental Group to summarize the findings detailed in *The Scole Report* for general readers. When you read this book, be aware that the full *Scole Report* is even more wonderful.

XV. Reincarnation

There is so much evidence for reincarnation that clearly something like it happens. It's a difficult process to understand, however, since time is not objectively real, so somehow all our lives on earth are happening at the same time. Accounts from upper-level beings suggest that we think of reincarnation not as a linear process, but more as a vat from which the bucket of each lifetime is dipped and back into which each lifetime is poured. Who knows? If you wonder about reincarnation, here are a few good books on the subject.

- *Reliving Past Lives* (1978) - Helen Wambach's groundbreaking study of mass hypnotic regressions is a brief and fascinating book. She set out to disprove reincarnation by hypnotically regressing thousands of people to lives lived in specific historical periods, expecting to be able to record an inconsistent mess of fantasy and gibberish. What she found instead was a distribution of thousands of memories of past lives that included genders, locations, clothing, utensils, foods, and other small details which so perfectly matched the historical record that to have achieved these results by chance was nearly mathematically impossible.

- *Twenty Cases Suggestive of Reincarnation* (1971); *Unlearned Language* (1984); *Where Reincarnation and Biology Intersect* (1997) - Ian Stevenson was Chairman of the Department of Psychiatry at the University of Virginia, and he was a leading researcher in the field of reincarnation. Stevenson spent a half-century studying cases of young children who remembered recent previous lives that had ended violently, and the result is a spectacular body of work which will be celebrated only when the rest of modern science catches up with it. Stevenson wrote for scientists, so his writing style is dry. But the work that he details in his dozen or more volumes is overwhelming evidence for prompt reincarnation in what appears to be the narrow case of unexpected violent death. These are three of his seminal works.

- *Many Lives, Many Masters* (1988); *Same Soul, Many Bodies* (2004) - Brian Weiss is the foremost popularizer of past-life regression therapy for use in the treatment of medical and psychological problems. An eminent Yale-trained psychiatrist, Weiss accidentally discovered the effect that apparent past lives can have on our present life. Unlike other regression therapists who have made the same discovery, he risked his medical career to get the word out. He has even ventured into the newer field of progression therapy (the investigation of how our future lives might affect the present one), which consciousness theory suggests should be possible, although it is a lot harder for us linear-thinking humans to grasp. The result is two illuminating books that offer a good introduction to the whole topic of reincarnation.
- *Children's Past Lives* (1997); *Return From Heaven* (2001) - Carol Bowman has studied the past-life memories of children, and while most of Stevenson's subjects remembered only their most recent lives, Bowman studied children whose present lives appeared to have been affected by traumas suffered in more distant lifetimes. She also has studied the phenomenon of children quickly reincarnating within the same family, which appears to happen fairly often when infants or toddlers die.
- *Reincarnation – The Missing Link in Christianity* (1997) - Elizabeth Clare Prophet wrote a scholarly but highly readable exposition of reincarnation as an original Christian belief. People who doubt that reincarnation was taught and believed by the earliest Christians owe it to themselves to read this book.
- *Your Soul's Plan* (2009) - Robert Schwartz wrote the definitive work on the fact that nearly all of us write life-plans before our births, and these can contain what we might consider to be

negative events. Understanding why sometimes very bad things happen for our own spiritual good can help us to make the most of crucial lessons, and might perhaps reduce the need for us to return for additional lifetimes.

XVI. Spirit Influence and Possession

You may or may not take seriously something for which there is considerable evidence: it seems to be possible for living people to be influenced or even possessed by spirits of the dead. Indeed, the condition may even be common, and it may be the cause of any number of otherwise inexplicable maladies. Who knows? Unlike mediumship and near-death experiences, possession has scarcely been studied at all, and spirit-releasement therapy is seldom practiced now because state regulators and malpractice insurers frown on it. This attitude can be expected to change once eternal Mind is shown to be the source of reality. Meanwhile, those few therapists who have made their careers in spirit-releasement therapy (the process of coaxing possessing beings away from their victims and toward the loved ones waiting for them) have had such apparent success that you may find these books fascinating.

- *People Who Don't Know They're Dead* (2005) - Gary Leon Hill wrote a quick and enjoyable book that is a useful introduction to the topic.
- *Healing Lost Souls* (2003) - William J. Baldwin was a late-twentieth-century expert in this field.

XVII. Achieving More Rapid Spiritual Growth

There have been a number of good things to come from the nascent science of afterlife studies, even beyond the obvious boon of our knowing at last that our minds are eternal. We also have learned from the dead why we even take lifetimes on earth at all: we come here to raise our personal spiritual vibrations away from fear and toward more perfect love, just as Jesus tells us is true in the Gospels. As the truth about reality becomes more widely known, and as our need to achieve rapid spiritual growth becomes foremost in more of the developed world, there will be many new resources to aid us. For now, here are some important books to help you in your quest for spiritual growth.

- *Matthew, Mark, Luke, and John* - The red letters in any modern translation of these four slim books of the Christian Bible are the only place where the words of Jesus are preserved. Early church councils edited the Gospels, both removing things that Jesus had said and adding bits about church-building, sheep-and-goats, and Apocalyptic warnings that Jesus could not have uttered; but otherwise the words of Jesus in the Gospels are amply corroborated by what the dead now tell us. Appendix III of The Fun of Dying, The Fun of Staying in Touch, and The Fun of Growing Forever gives you further details about the correspondences between the genuine teachings of Jesus and the modern afterlife evidence.
- *Awaken with Gratitude* (2016) - Hillis Pugh is a guru of gratitude. He teaches it, and he can help you understand how to use it to its best effect.
- *The Fun of Growing Forever – We Can't Transform the World Until We Transform Ourselves* (2016, 2021) - Roberta Grimes uses the teachings of Jesus to deliver the simplest and among the most effective methods for achieving rapid spiritual growth while we go on living our daily lives.
- *Conscious Being* (2015) - TJ Woodward's book rocked my world. Here are the essential Gospel teachings, arrived at from the perspective of Eastern writings! TJ writes beautifully and very accessibly. If you really cannot stand to think of doing anything related to the Bible, then perhaps his book will be enough for you; although once you have begun to work on

forgiveness, I hope you will soon realize that you also need to forgive Christianity.

- *A Course in Miracles* (1992, 2008, 2009) - Helen Schucman with the help of William Thetford received between 1965 and 1972 this set of Text, Workbook for Students, and Manual for Teachers that apparently was channeled by a team that Jesus led. Wherever the *Course* came from, it is a powerful set of lessons in ultimate forgiveness. If you are ready to try for Level Six of the afterlife realities at the end of this lifetime, then doing the *Course* may be your best shot! Beware, though. The *Course* is heavy learning, and it is very hard to manage on your own. Fortunately, there are *A Course in Miracles* study groups in most cities worldwide.

- *Quantum Forgiveness* (2015) - David Hoffmeister is a student of A Course in Miracles who uses movies as modern-day parables to give us another approach to learning forgiveness.

- *Liberating Jesus* (2015, 2021) - Roberta Grimes received this book during two weeks of time from an entity who reportedly was Jesus. Many of those who have fallen away from strict Christian practice love *Liberating Jesus*, although for devout Christians what it has to say about the religion can be troubling to read.

Appendix III

Listening to Jesus

This information is meant for Christians who are coming to accept what the afterlife evidence tells us is true, but remain devoted to the teachings of Jesus. If you are not a Christian, please skip this Appendix. I have no wish to interfere with your religious beliefs.

I was a devout Christian for most of my life. For me, the hardest thing to accept about the afterlife evidence was the fact that it so blatantly contradicts some of the teachings of mainstream Christianity. It was only when I re-read the Gospel words of Jesus in light of what I had learned from the afterlife evidence that I realized that two thousand years ago, Jesus shared with us truths about God, reality, death, the afterlife, and the meaning and purpose of human life that we could not have confirmed independently until the twentieth century. Thanks to modern afterlife communications, now we can prove that Jesus is real! He tells us repeatedly in the Gospels that he came as our teacher, and at last we can begin to see what he meant to teach.

The afterlife evidence indicates that a lot of what mainstream Christianity teaches is based in human ideas. The dead don't sleep until they hear a final trumpet. Their bodies don't reassemble out of the soil. Being baptized does not matter after death; having taken communion does not matter; and accepting Jesus as our personal savior makes no discernible afterlife difference. Evidence suggests that practicing any religion in life does not matter after death, but what counts for us when we die is our having lived our lives in close accordance with Jesus's Gospel teachings.

Jesus tells us to **"Ask, and it will be given to you; seek, and you will find"** (LK 9:11). So I asked. I urge you to do the same! And I see this as a matter of some urgency now, since the afterlife realities are as real as this material universe. As good communications are developed between this material level and the higher frequency levels where most of the dead reside, it will become clear that mainstream Christianity has not been teaching what is factual. If believers begin to turn away from Christianity, we don't want them also turning away from Jesus.

Reading Jesus's Gospel Teachings

Think how extraordinary it is that we have the two-thousand-year-old words of someone who claimed to understand reality, and to know what happens when we die. Now add the fact that most of what Jesus says in the Gospels is consistent with what we can only now deduce from afterlife evidence and cutting-edge science. This gives us some amazing validations of both the teachings of Jesus and the modern evidence! Such an extensive coincidence is so unlikely as to be for practical purposes impossible. Yet if you share my wonder and delight at finding how well the words of Jesus fit the evidence, I have to remind you that the odds are long against our having available to us exactly what he said.

Many Christians consider the entire Bible to be the Inspired Word of God. Having read it through a number of times, I must tell you that I find the Bible to be so internally inconsistent and so full of culturally biased and even un-Christian advice that it seems presumptuous and insulting to pin it all on God. It seems more accurate to say that the writers whose work was assembled into the Christian Bible may have been inspired by God, but they heard

God through the filter of their primitive lives in the ancient world, so they could have garbled some of God's message. This would be understandable and forgivable. But the fact that it might have happened means that no serious researcher can use most of the Bible as a resource when trying to understand a factual God.

The red letters of the Gospels are another matter. Thomas Jefferson said that the words of Jesus stand out in the Bible like "diamonds in a dunghill," and when you read the Bible through and reach the Gospels, you can see what he meant. In a recent translation, Jesus sounds like a modern man trying to educate primitives: you see him speaking simply and patiently, saying things over and over to people who seem not really to understand him. You even see his rising frustration, and his repeated efforts to quell that frustration and say things over yet again, more simply. Put aside the fact that Jesus's followers started in his name a prominent and now widely-fragmented religion. Just read the words of Jesus without religious bias, and you find yourself sympathizing and liking him as a wonderfully wise and good man you would enjoy having as your friend. Reading his words without religious bias makes you wonder whether things that he said might be found to be factually accurate.

Here is where our problems arise. If we don't want to indulge in the magic-thinking notion that the whole Bible is the Inspired Word of God, then we have to take into account how easily the teachings of Jesus could have been distorted during the past two thousand years:

1.   **For Jesus to speak against the prevailing religion was a crime punishable by death.** He was trying to stay alive long enough to share what he had come to teach, and he managed that feat for more than three years by using some fascinating tricks. He would tell what sounded like innocent stories, then say, "he who has ears to hear, let him hear" (wink-

wink) to urge his followers to look for his deeper messages. He would give people innocuous-sounding bits of information at various spots along the way, knowing that the guards watching him would change, and hoping that his faithful followers would be able to put those bits together.

2.   **Iron-age people who heard Jesus speak and passed his words along, and those who eventually committed them to writing, may not have fully understood what he was saying.** It is possible that they inserted or altered words or passages here and there to better support their own understandings. We would be none the wiser.

3.   **Jesus's message could have been altered as it was translated into Greek and then from Greek into English.** Aramaic is so different from Greek that direct translations from Aramaic to English are nearly unrecognizable by people who are used to modern Bible versions. The fact that the Gospel words of Jesus that have been translated twice still are so consistent with the afterlife evidence is flat-out amazing to me.

4.   **We depend on the good will of those who were in control of the written Gospels for two millennia.** Here is where our trust is tested! There is evidence that people eager to support their own religious doctrines edited the Gospels over the years, which means that apparently words were put into or taken out of Jesus's mouth. This, too, makes the close correspondence between the surviving Gospel words of Jesus and modern afterlife communications a source of wonder and delight for me.

A few of Jesus's Gospel words are lumps of coal among the diamonds. He talks about a fiery hell; he calls Peter the rock on which he will build his church. These passages are inconsistent with afterlife-related evidence, and also with the rest of Jesus's Gospel teachings, which leads me to believe they are doctrinal edits. If we ignore these atypical bits, then what we have left in all four Gospels is a message that is stunningly consistent with the modern afterlife evidence. The man clearly knew what he was talking about, since his words agree with modern evidence in ways that could not have been known—and, indeed, might not have been liked—by the people who preserved them.

Let us imagine that we are only now finding the Gospel words of Jesus, and we know nothing about the religion that was later established in his name. We can see from afterlife-related evidence that two thousand years ago Jesus was familiar with facts about God, reality, death the afterlife, and the meaning and purpose of human life that have come to light only recently. If all that we had were his newly found teachings, the afterlife evidence, and the afterlife science, how might we now interpret Jesus's words?

He Taught Us About God

Jesus told us the fundamental fact that God is loving Spirit, and each of us is part of God. This was radical stuff in ancient times, when most people worshiped semi-physical gods who were more like the Old Testament's Jehovah, often vengeful and hard to placate.

"God is spirit, and his worshipers must worship in spirit and in truth." (JN 4:24)

"The kingdom of God is within you." (LK 17:20–21)

"The Spirit gives life; the flesh counts for nothing. The words I have spoken to you are spirit, and they are life." (JN 6:63)

"If you love me, you will obey what I command. And he will ask the Father, and he will give you another Counselor to be with you forever—the Spirit of truth. The world cannot accept him, because it neither sees him nor knows him. But you know him, for he lives with you and will be in you." (JN 14:15–17)

Jesus took the ancient Hebrews' radical concept of a single nonphysical God and transformed it into what modern evidence shows us is universal Spirit (or Mind).

He Taught Us the Importance of Love

Jesus reduced the Old Testament's Ten Commandments to one commandment: that we learn how to love.

"A new command I give you: Love one another. As I have loved you, so you must love one another." (JN 13:34)

"'Love the Lord your God with all your heart and with all your soul and with all your mind.' This is the first and greatest commandment. And the second is like it: 'Love your neighbor as yourself.' All the Law and the Prophets hang on these two commandments." (MT 22:37–40)

"You have heard that it was said, 'Love your neighbor and hate your enemy.' But I tell you: love your enemies and pray for those who persecute you, that you may be sons of your Father in heaven . . . . Be perfect, therefore, as your heavenly Father is perfect." (MT 5:43–48)

He Taught Us the Importance of Forgiveness

When I first realized that God does not judge us, I worried that on this point Jesus might have been mistaken. But then I considered this series of quotations.

"For if you forgive men when they sin against you, your heavenly Father will also forgive you. But if you do not forgive men their sins, your Father will not forgive your sins." (MT 6:14–15)

"Moreover, the Father judges no one, but has entrusted all judgment to the Son, that all may honor the Son just as they honor the Father." (JN 5:21–23)

"You judge by human standards; I pass judgment on no one." (JN 8:15)

"As for the person who hears my words but does not keep them, I do not judge him. For I did not come to judge the world, but to save it." (JN 12:47)

Were these messages inconsistencies? I think not. Instead, I think they were Jesus's efforts (meted out in bits at different times beneath the Temple's radar) to wean his primitive listeners from their old idea of God as judge so they could better comprehend what modern evidence tells us is true: each of us will be our own post-death judge. Jesus's disciple, Peter, asked him, "Lord, how many times shall I forgive my brother when he sins against me? Up to seven times?" Jesus answered, **"I tell you, not seven times, but seventy-seven times"** (MT 18:21–23). He even hinted pretty strongly that each of us will judge ourselves:

"Do not judge, or you too will be judged. For in the same way you judge others, you will be judged, and with the measure you use, it will be measured to you." (MT 7:1–2).

He Taught Us the Need for Humility

Into that ancient class-obsessed world Jesus brought a rude shock for the elite: after we die, our status in life means nothing.

"Many who are first will be last, and the last first." (MK 10:31)

"The greatest among you will be your servant. For whoever exalts himself will be humbled, and whoever humbles himself will be exalted." (MT 23:11–12)

"Whoever welcomes this little child in my name welcomes me, and whoever welcomes me welcomes the one who sent me. For he who is least among you all—he is the greatest." (LK 9:48)

"Let the little children come to me, and do not hinder them, for the kingdom of God belongs to such as these. I tell you the truth, anyone who will not receive The kingdom of God like a little child will never enter it." (MK 10:14–15)

He Taught Us About the Power of Our Minds

Mainstream Christian doctrines ignore something that strikes a modern nonreligious reader: Jesus said a lot about the power of our minds to affect reality.

"Take heart, daughter. Your faith has healed you." (MT 9:22)

(healing a blind man) "Do you believe that I am able to do this? . . . According to your faith will it be done to you." (MT 9:28–29)

(When Peter couldn't walk on water) "You of little faith. Why did you doubt?" (MT 14:31)

"Who touched me? Someone touched me. I know that power has gone out from me . . . Daughter, your faith has healed you. Go in peace." (LK 8:46–48)

"Have faith in God. I tell you the truth, if anyone says to this mountain, 'Go, throw yourself into the sea,' and does not doubt in his heart but believes that what he says will happen, it will be done for him. Therefore I tell you, whatever you ask for in prayer, believe that you have received it, and it will be yours." (MK 11:22–24)

It is difficult for us to appreciate how radical these teachings were in the Judea and Samaria of two thousand years ago. Jesus used the familiar Hebrew concept of faith in God to teach his followers the power of their eternal minds, and to teach them that their minds—like his—were part of one universal Mind.

"When you pray, go into your room, close the door and pray to your Father, who is unseen. Then your Father, who sees what is done in secret, will reward you." (MT 6:6)

"For whatever is hidden is meant to be disclosed, and whatever is concealed is meant to be brought out into the open. If anyone has ears to hear, let him hear." (MK 4:22–23)

He Taught Us About the Afterlife

Some of the messages attributed to Jesus seem inexplicable and even cruel until we compare them with the afterlife evidence. That is when we realize that Jesus was talking not about this life, but about the afterlife. He was right in telling us that spiritual development is our real goal, and right in saying there is no way to short-cut it. He was right, too, in saying that those who don't progress sufficiently may regress and lose whatever progress they have made, even judging and condemning themselves to the dark and smelly lowest afterlife level, which he referred to as the outer darkness.

"For everyone who has will be given more, and he will have an abundance. Whoever does not have, even what he has will be taken from him. And throw that worthless servant outside, into the darkness, where there will be weeping and gnashing of teeth." (MT 29:30)

"For there is nothing hidden that will not be disclosed, and nothing concealed that will not be known or brought out into the open. Therefore consider carefully how you listen. Whoever has will be given more; whoever does not have, even what he thinks he has will be taken from him." (LK 8:17–18)

When Jesus mentions "having" in these places, he isn't talking about material things. He is referring to spiritual growth, which from his perspective is the one thing worth having.

Jesus told us about the tremendous size of the afterlife. He told us about our eternal progress. He even told us that our loved ones would create after-death homes for us, and would meet us at our deaths and take us there.

"In my father's house are many rooms; if it were not so, I would have told you. I am going there to prepare a place for you. And if I go and prepare a place for you, I will come back and take you to be with me that you also may be where I am. You know the way to the place where I am going." (JN 14:2–4)

"Blessed are the poor in spirit, for theirs is the kingdom of heaven . . . . Blessed are the pure in heart, for they will see God." (MT 5:3, 8)

His Teachings Are a Prescription for Spiritual Advancement

The law of spiritual advancement is implacable. Contrary to modern Christian teachings about "salvation" resulting from the death of Jesus, Jesus himself is exactly right: there are no shortcuts. Much of what Jesus says in the Gospels can be read as lessons in better controlling your mind.

"Do not resist an evil person. If someone strikes you on the right cheek, turn to him the other also. And if someone wants to sue you and take your tunic, let him have your cloak as well. If someone forces you to go one mile, go with him two miles." (MT 5:39–1)

"You have heard that it was said to the people long ago, 'Do not murder, and anyone who murders will be subject to judgment.' But I tell you that anyone who is angry with his brother will be subject to judgment. Again, anyone who says to his brother, 'Raca,' is answerable to the Sanhedrin. But anyone who says, 'You fool' will be in danger of the fire of hell." (MT 5:21–22)

"Why do you look at the speck of sawdust in your brother's eye and pay no attention to the plank in your own eye? How can you say to your brother, 'Brother, let me take the speck out of your eye,' when you yourself fail to see the plank in your own eye? You hypocrite, first take the plank out of your eye, and then you will see clearly to remove the speck from your brother's eye." (LK 6:41–42)

"If any one of you is without sin, let him be the first to throw a stone at her." (JN 8:7)

"But love your enemies, do good to them, and lend to them without expecting to get anything back. Then your reward will be great, and you will be sons of the Most High, because he is kind to the ungrateful and wicked. Be merciful, just as your Father is merciful." (LK 6:35–36)

Jesus shared wonderful parables about spiritual growth. We know them as the tales of the Good Samaritan, the Keeper of the Vineyard, and the Prodigal Son. In every way that he could, he urged his listeners to keep striving for spiritual perfection.

"I tell you that in the same way there is more rejoicing in heaven over one sinner who repents than over ninety-nine righteous persons who do not need to repent." (LK 15:7)

He Did Not Like Clergymen or Religious Traditions

Jesus was kind to everyone. He loved even lepers and tax collectors, at a time when lepers were shunned by all and tax collectors were evil incarnate. The only people who griped him were clergymen. He was bothered by not just their fake piety and self-importance, but also their religious traditions.

"Watch out for the teachers of the law. They like to walk around in flowing robes and be greeted in the marketplaces, and have the most important seats in the synagogues and the places of honor at banquets. They devour widows' houses and for a show make lengthy prayers. Such men will be punished most severely." (MK 12:38–40)

"And why do you break the command of God for the sake of your tradition? You hypocrites! Isaiah was right when he prophesied about you: 'These people honor me with their lips, but their hearts are far from me. They worship me in vain; their teachings are but rules taught by men.'" (MT 15:3–9)

"You have let go of the commands of God and are holding on to the traditions of men . . . You have a fine way of setting aside the commands of God in order to observe your own traditions." (MK 7:8–9)

"Be careful not to do your 'acts of righteousness' before men, to be seen by them. If you do, you will have no reward from your Father in heaven. So when you give to the needy, do not announce it with trumpets, as the hypocrites do in the synagogues and on the streets, to be honored by men. I tell you the truth, they have received their reward in full. But when you give to the needy, do not let your left hand know what your right hand is doing, so that your giving may be in secret. Then your father, who sees what is done in secret, will reward you. When you pray, do not be like the hypocrites, for they love to pray standing in the synagogues and on the street corners to be seen by men. I tell you the truth, they have received their reward in full. When you pray, go into your room, close the door and pray to your Father, who is unseen. Then your Father, who sees what is done in secret, will reward you." (MT 6:1–6)

Does this sound like someone who was trying to establish his own religion? Or was he instead telling us that we don't need religions at all, but we can approach God individually, since each of us is part of universal Mind?

Jesus's teachings are profoundly individual.

"Ask, and it will be given to you; seek, and you will find; knock, and the door will be opened to you. For everyone who asks receives; he who seeks finds; and to him who knocks, the door is opened." (LK 11:9–10)

"Not everyone who says to me, 'Lord, Lord,' will enter the kingdom of heaven, but only he who does the will of my Father who is in heaven." (MT 7:21)

"Why do you call me 'Lord, Lord,' and do not do what I say?" (LK 6:46)

"If you hold to my teaching, you are really my disciples. Then you will know the truth, and the truth will set you free." (JN 8:31–32)

It amazes me that so little has been made of the fact that this perfectly loving man seems to have had an aversion to religions. Does it not seem possible that, far from establishing yet one more religion, Jesus was trying to "set you free" from religions altogether?

His Death Was Not Meant to Save Us From God's Wrath

I have a confession to make. I have always found it hard to believe that an infinitely loving God would demand the blood-sacrifice of His own child. Whenever I asked clergymen about it, they would say it was "a sacred mystery." I know better now. **The afterlife evidence tells us that accepting Jesus as one's personal savior is not necessary for salvation, and neither God nor any religious figure ever is our afterlife judge.** So if Jesus didn't die as a blood-sacrifice to redeem us from God's punishment for our sins, then what else might have been the purpose of his dramatic death and resurrection?

Perhaps it was an exclamation point. Perhaps he was demonstrating for simple people the good news that death is not real.

Jesus's Message Is Not That Being a Christian Is the Only Way to Salvation

As Christianity developed, Christians became convinced that Jesus had said that accepting him as one's personal savior was the only way to heaven.

"I am the way, the truth and the life. No one comes to the Father except through me." (JN 14:6)

"I am the resurrection and the life. He who believes in me will live, even though he dies; and whoever lives and believes in me will never die." (JN 11:25–26)

Modern evidence does not support this Christians-only reading of his words, but it would support another reading. Simply replace "I" and "me" with "my teachings":

"My teachings are the way, the truth and the life. No one comes to the Father except through my teachings."

"My teachings are the resurrection and the life. He who believes in my teachings will live, even though he dies; and whoever lives and believes in my teachings will never die."

Jesus so persistently emphasized our need to follow his *teachings* that this revised reading makes more sense. Perhaps those who heard him misunderstood him, or perhaps later custodians of his words altered them to better support developing Christian doctrines. Unfortunately, in reliance on those altered words, Jesus's followers soon were torturing and murdering and committing mayhem in his name, in utter contravention of his teachings. No conversion effort has been considered too brutal to be used, if making people Christian was the only way to "save" them.

But Jesus told us repeatedly that following his *teachings* is what matters!

"What do you think? There was a man who had two sons. He went to the first and said, 'Son, go and work today in the vineyard.' 'I will not,' he answered, but later he changed his mind and went. Then the father went to the other son and said the same thing. He answered, 'I will, sir,' but he did not go. Which of the two did what his father wanted? . . . I tell you the truth, the tax collectors and the prostitutes are entering the kingdom of God ahead of you." (MT 21:28–31)

"I say to you that many will come from the east and the west, and will take their places at the feast with Jacob in the kingdom of heaven. But the subjects of the kingdom will be thrown outside, into the darkness, where there will be weeping and gnashing of teeth." (MT 8:11–12)

Most comforting of all his words are these:

"I shall be with you always, to the very end of the age." (MT 28:20)

What Was His Mission?

Jesus was speaking to primitive people steeped in superstitious terrors and ignorant of nearly everything that you and I consider commonplace. His teachings for them were simple, even simplistic. We severely underestimate the man if we suppose that if he walked the earth today, he would express himself to us as he expressed himself to them. If we keep this fact in mind, then in light of modern afterlife evidence we can develop a pretty good sense of what Jesus was trying to do.

I think Jesus's life had a four-fold purpose.

First, he came to tell us what God is.

Second, he came to show us that life is eternal.

Third, he came to give us a taste of what the afterlife is like.

Finally, he came to teach us how to make the most spiritual progress while on Earth.

If these were his objectives, then his death and resurrection can be seen as a loving and joyous **"Ta-da!"**

Human beings were ready to start to learn what modern afterlife evidence has only now revealed to us, two very bloody millennia later. Had his followers fully understood what he was saying at the time, human history could have been so different!

Mainstream Christianity does not own Jesus, just as no religion owns God. Surely he deserves another chance to be heard in light of modern afterlife evidence. Paul and the other New Testament writers did a good job of wrapping Jesus's teachings in Hebrew prophesy so they could be preserved for two thousand years. **Thank you, Paul! Now at last we can open your gift.**

Appendix IV

Experiences of Light

My lifelong interest in death is an offshoot of something that happened in April of 1955. One morning I woke up just before dawn and was struck by the thought that there is no God. I stared in terror into the darkness, too full of despair even to seek the comfort of my parents' bed. What comfort can there be if there is no God?

Suddenly there was a flash of white light in the room. I could look at it without squinting, and even more than sixty years later I still recall the wonder of seeing light shining on my toy horse, on my plastic dolls in a row, and on that awful lavender wallpaper. **In the midst of the flash, I heard a young male voice say, "You wouldn't know what it is to have me unless you knew what it is to be without me. I will never leave you again."**

Almost forty years went by before I told anyone what had happened to me, but it shaped my growing-up. Surely my experience had been normal. I assumed that I was going to learn about experiences of light at church or in school or somewhere. I even majored in religion in college, but of course all that I learned in college was what the world's great religions had taught. By my junior year, I was starting to think that my experience would be a mystery forever. Then one August day as I was turning twenty, I came home from my summer job and sat down on my bed, feeling glum.

Suddenly there it was again, the magnesium-white light filling the room, this time accompanied by indescribable music. Think of a thousand tiny bells playing beautifully and loudly. Then came that same young male voice, this time saying only, **"I will never leave you."**

Never for a minute since that day have I thought that I was alone, and never have I doubted the existence of God. And for many years, I was convinced that I was the literal dunce of the universe, since God had to make His point to me twice. I was so embarrassed that for years I swore to God that I always would remember that He was real, **"so please don't ever do that to me again!"** In all the years since, God never has.

For nearly four decades I lived with the thought that the only three people who had been spoken to from out of a flash of light were Moses, the Apostle Paul, and a dumbfounded American child.

Here is what happened to Moses:

"The angel of the Lord appeared to him in a blazing fire from the midst of a bush; and he looked, and behold, the bush was burning with fire, yet the bush was not consumed. So Moses said, **'I must turn aside now and see this marvelous sight, why the bush is not burned up.'**

"When the Lord saw that he turned aside to look, God called to him from the midst of the bush and said, **'Moses, Moses!'**

"And he said, **'Here I am.'**

"Then He said, 'Do not come near here; remove your sandals from your feet, for the place on which you are standing is holy ground'" (Exodus 3:2–5).

And here is how a zealot named Saul was converted after the death of Jesus from a persecutor of those who had followed the Lord into the Apostle Paul, the architect of the early Church:

"Now Saul, still breathing threats and murder against the disciples of the Lord, went to the high priest, and asked for letters from him to the synagogues at Damascus, so that if he found any belonging to the Way, both men and women, he might bring them bound to Jerusalem. As he was traveling, it happened that he was approaching Damascus, and suddenly a light from heaven flashed around him; and he fell to the ground and heard a voice saying to him, **'Saul, Saul, why are you persecuting Me?'**

"And he said, **'Who are You, Lord?'**

"And He said, **'I am Jesus whom you are persecuting, but get up and enter the city, and it will be told you what you must do'"** (Acts 9:1–6).

These great religious figures had conversed with the voices they had heard from the light. For my part, when I saw the light and heard the voice, my only thought was that it was handy that if you forget there is a God, they remind you. But until I was forty-five, I never heard of anyone else outside the Bible who had had an experience of light.

Then my father had a major stroke. For the two weeks that he survived, I made a daily round trip to be with my parents, and on one of those nights my mother had essentially my same experience. She saw a flash of white light, and a voice said, **"I'm giving you a few more days with him so you can get a few things straight."**

(Nobody said these great experiences have to be poetic.)

It was only after I discovered that they had not been unique to me that I began to mention my experiences of light. I have found that a few of those with whom I have shared my experiences have had similar experiences themselves, and they generally don't talk about them, either. This is something so personal, so extraordinary, and frankly so weird that you don't talk about it. But it is something that stays in your mind. I have no other memories from the spring when I was eight, but still that predawn minute shines.

As to what makes an experience of light look and sound as it does, here are my thoughts:

- All the post-death levels exist right here, and the third level and above are filled with a white light that is brighter than sunlight. Opening a portal between our levels might leak that light through briefly, which I have come to think is what happens.

- Most people who have experiences of light have the same sense that I did: the light is in the room, but the voice and music may be in your mind.

- Experiences of light seem to occur when we are under some spiritual strain, and most of the messages that have been shared with me were spiritual in nature.

- People differ on who it was they thought they heard speaking, and by their descriptions I have come to guess that we all hear different voices. The voice that I heard was young and male and it didn't seem quite God-like, so when in my research I encountered spirit guides, I realized that my voice must have been my spirit guide. My mother was certain that she had heard the literal voice of God Himself, and I find it interesting that as her brain deteriorated with end-stage senile dementia, her experience of light was the last thing she forgot, even when she no longer recognized her children.

- To hear a voice in your mind as clearly as you hear spoken words is a remarkable experience. I assure you that you can tell the difference between spoken words and your own thoughts. No question.

Having lived successfully for decades after I had my last experience of light, having married and reared children and practiced law and made friends, I am demonstrably not crazy. But I am so glad that at the age of eight I knew enough not to tell anyone what had happened to me! Now I wonder how many others have been made to consider themselves insane because they had this sort of wonderful cross-dimensional message, and the doctors they trusted with it decided that they had to be mad. I have come to think that many things that mainstream scientists still find puzzling may have their origins in the afterlife levels, which is another reason why I hope that soon they can get past their beliefs-based views of what reality must be.

ISBN 9781737410621

51695 >

Milton Keynes UK
Ingram Content Group UK Ltd.
UKHW020632140923
428670UK00014B/726